Glasgow Central on 9 June 1956 with 46236 CITY OF BRADFORD setting back onto its train which would be the morning Glasgow-Birmingham. This train followed the up 'Royal Scot' which can be seen waiting to depart at Platform 1 on the extreme right. Although it cannot be positively identified the 'Royal Scot' engine is a Polmadie one as the first four numbers are 4622 and this engine would work the train to Carlisle. The other engine however, 46236, Camden based, would work through to Crewe as part of a cyclic diagram. Contrary to the rules the engine already carries the class one train headcode lamps.

CITY OF LEEDS at Preston on 12 June 1963 and in the process of shunting some vans. Judging by the headcode the engine was working a class 3 van train and is probably either detaching or adding vehicles. By this date the engine is in maroon livery with BR style lining and fitted with a speedometer and AWS equipment. Photograph A.W. Battson, www.tranporttreasury.co.uk

The Book of the
CORONATION PACIFICS

By
Ian Sixsmith

CITY OF BRADFORD, with it own tender properly lettered BRITISH RAILWAYS, in Sonning Cutting on the Western Region, a presage of times to come, when Stanier Pacifics (two Princesses, 46207 and 46210 and two Coronations, 46254 and 46257) would go to Old Oak in 1956 to substitute for Kings with bogie troubles. See pages 30-31. Photograph Maurice Earley, National Railway Museum.

Cover photograph: Polmadie, Glasgow. J.Robertson, B.P. Hoper Collection.

From the front, all hint of bulbousness disappeared; it was grace and power. This is 6220 CORONATION storming out of London on 29 June 1937 with the famous trial run for the press, Euston to Crewe. It was only two miles from Crewe that the train touched 114mph, with Crewe North's Tommy Clark at the regulator. It was F.A. Lemon, the Crewe Works man who, sitting opposite Stanier (according to H.A.V. Bulleid in *Master Builders of Steam*) put his legs on the seat opposite in preparation for what he saw as the inevitable derailment. Stanier kept his aplomb, but considered they had been saved from disaster by the de Glehn bogie. Photograph G.W. Goslin Collection.

Copyright Irwell Press &
Ian Sixsmith
ISBN 1-871608-94-5

Contents

Some Background

'Stanier was the man to get our locomotive programme straightened out'

Page 1

Some Changes and Differences

'the engines have proved highly successful, and the percentage of punctual arrivals at each end has been uniformly high'

Page 17

The Record

46220 - 46257

Page 33

An Appendix

From the Horse's Mouth

Page 97

CORONATION with the inaugural Coronation Scot, leaving Euston on 5 July 1937. The stock was conventional, but repainted and refitted. Despite the glorious non-stop test runs of Princess Royal Pacific 6201 PRINCESS ELIZABETH in the previous autumn, intended to provide data for the proposed Coronation Scot, the timing for the new train was set at only 6½ hours in each direction, with a stop at Carlisle. PRINCESS ELIZABETH had worked non-stop Euston to Glasgow on 16 November 1936 and back the next day. The schedule was six hours but this was cut by some minutes on both trips.

First Published
in the United Kingdom by
IRWELL PRESS 1998
59A, High Street,
Clophill,
Bedfordshire MK45 4BE
Printed & Bound by The Amadeus Press,
Cleckheaton, West Yorkshire.

You'll Remember those Black and White Days...

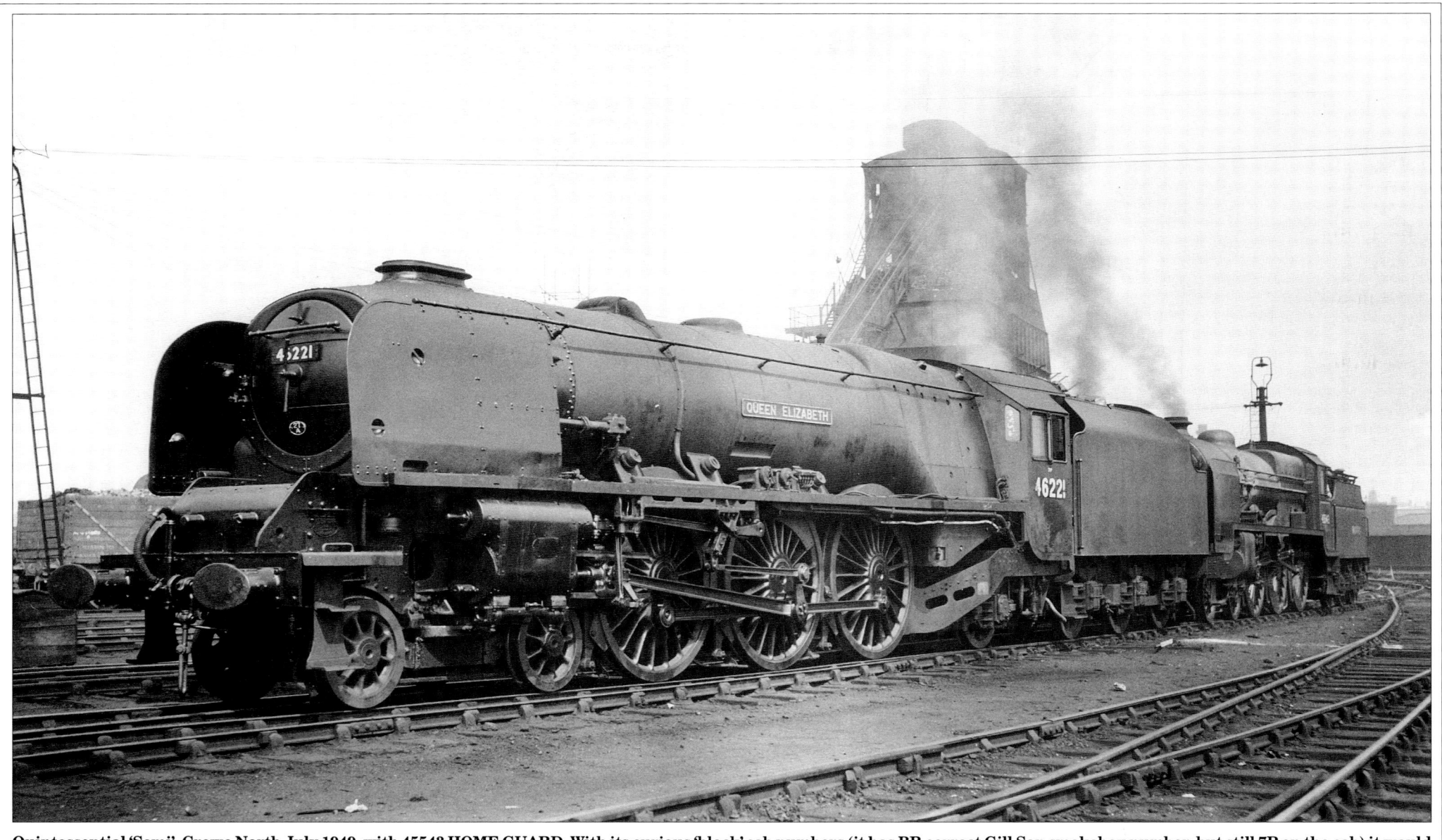

Quintessential 'Semi', Crewe North July 1949, with 45543 HOME GUARD. With its curious 'block' cab numbers (it has BR correct Gill San smokebox number, but still 7P on the cab) it would be in the post-war LMS lined black, though grime covers any trace of lining. The smokebox has had a good going over but the tender is filthy, suggesting 46221 is ex-works after some untoward or Intermediate repair. Under a glass the original print reveals the 4 of the cab number to be a feebler, undersized numeral compared to the original 6221. QUEEN ELIZABETH had lost her streamlined case in the period ending 13 July 1946 and was renumbered 46221 week ending 23 October 1948. Note small cab window, soon to be enlarged—this can be compared to conventional and other 'de-streamlined' engines. Photograph W. Hermiston, B.P. Hoper Collection.

SOME BACKGROUND

'Stanier was the man to get our locomotive programme straightened out'

The streamliners were a PR man's dream—the Great Western lined up Kings at Swindon and the LNER lined up A4s for *Picture Post*-type spreads but few locomotives had such dramatic, PR-friendly outlines as the new Stanier Pacifics. This was the traditional place for the LMS publicity shot, outside the Paint Shop at Crewe; indeed the LM became so attached to the practice that it even lined up new Ivatt 2-6-0s, hardly the visual equivalents of the streamliners—see *British Railways Illustrated* Vol.1 No.2, December 1991. The glittering trio is made up of the three new engines of June 1937: 6220 CORONATION, 6221 QUEEN ELIZABETH and 6222 QUEEN MARY.

Stanier's range of standard locomotives has come to personify the LMS, and the thinking and practice that suffused it carried over into the Standard locomotives of British Railways. The BR Standards, though they incorporated much advantageous detail work from the other companies' traditions, owed their lineage above all to the LMS, and the rebirth of its locomotive engineering under Stanier.

It all would have been very different but for the chance vagaries of history. George Hughes had succeeded to the office of CME on the conjoining of the L&Y and the LNWR to form a 'super-company' in 1922, anticipating the Grouping of a year later. Schooled in the principles of standardisation, Hughes announced a scheme of six classes for the combined company and after Grouping this was expanded to twelve. E.S. Cox outlined these in 1924 but, as is recorded abundantly elsewhere, only the 5ft.6in. 'Crab' (there was also a planned 5ft.1in. 2-6-0) appeared, in May 1926. Hughes had retired in the autumn of 1925 and 'the Horwich Mogul' was the only design sufficiently advanced so that it could not be cancelled or 'Midlandised' out of existence by the

Derby camp, the coming force in the LMS mechanical landscape, and set to remain so for the rest of the 1920s.

Stanier was appointed from 1 January 1932 and a charming account of his 'head hunting' (as it would be termed today) is given by H.A.V. Bulleid in his book *Master Builders of Steam* (Ian Allan, 1963). 'Cloak and daggerish' invitations to London clubs were (very properly) reported by Stanier to his boss Collett, who gave his blessing. (Stanier at 55 was only five years younger than Collett, and thus poorly placed to make a mark if the expected succession occurred and nothing untoward took place.) Sir

Euston was a funny place. You could go there and not see a *single* Pacific; I can still recall the keen-ness of a ten year-old's disappointment even now, several centuries later. But Euston was like unwrapping a dainty; here is the famous Propylaeum from some doorway opposite. Beyond that great Doric doorway were further doorways and passages, finally leading to the treasure within...

A bit of fun in the wind tunnel. Photograph National Railway Museum.

Harold Hartley of the LMS spoke with Stanier, together with Sir Ernest Lemon, who was briefly a 'caretaker' CME after Fowler, before moving on to be Vice President. Hartley is quoted as deciding that *'Stanier was the man to get our locomotive programme straightened out. The number of different types we had inherited was appalling...'*

And this nearly a decade after the company's foundation! Without doubt, these sentiments would have been put to Stanier, though he would hardly have entered the discussions at the Athenaeum and the Traveller's Club without having a fairly shrewd idea of how locomotive matters were going on the Great Western's huge rival. From the desperation

expressed by Hartley, it is not hard to see the origins of the clout Stanier wielded on the LMS. He would have declared to Lemon and Hartley that he needed to carry though something of a revolution, and would never have left Swindon without assurances that there was full backing for such a campaign. Stanier duly made his way to the LMS and began the great task; 'Augean' would be to make far too much of it, though Bulleid's odd but attractive phrase, 'mighty re-stocking' captures it precisely.

Cox's scheme of 1924 had included a Pacific and Fowler, too, had come up with plans for a sort of 'super-Compound' 4-6-2. Stanier's first locomotive (what he thought of the 0-4-4Ts, already underway and

coming out in 1932, his first full year of office, would be a treasure) was a 2-6-0, in which he wrestled the big, 'partly-Midland', parallel boiler 'Crab' into the taper boiler world of The Way Ahead. The Crab had been very successful, for it was a modern and forward-looking piece of work; it shone, moreover, against some of the designs going into service around it, such as the 0-6-0 and the 0-8-0.

Stanier's aim in producing this 2-6-0, it seems, was to stamp the principle of the new order straight away, and a request from the Operating people for 'more Crabs' was a convenient way of doing it. Taper boilers were the most marked departure from time-honoured practice and Stanier was thereafter

The Stanier/de Glehn bogie(or rather Churchward/de Glehn, for it was an exact replica of the GW 4-cylinder loco bogie) that proved so useful on the occasion of CORONATION's 114mph dash, on 29 June 1937. The streamliner under construction next door is almost certainly 6220 itself and this then would be its first bogie (they did get swapped around a bit). This is 'No.1 Belt' in Ten Shop at Crewe and the Super D across the way is on 'No.2 Belt'. At this time 'No.1' was the 'new work' belt.

New wheels on the balancing machine at Crewe Wheel Shop, 1937. The weight of the balancing is being calculated; the motor on the right will spin the wheelset, and the 'ship's wheel' at the front is for braking—note the shoes operated off it. Note also the weights on inside and outside cranks to simulate the weight of the connecting rods. This is a leading wheelset and, judging by the size, off a Pacific. It cannot be a Princess as there are no eccentric sheaves, so it must be a 'big 'un'. The spring loaded attachments around the axle journals would be used to measure the degree to which the set was 'out of balance' and lead would be put between the balance weight plates, riveted between the spokes, until the required balance was achieved. These side plates don't appear to have been fitted yet.

set to establish his rite of passage. This, as for any new CME, was always the same - the newest and latest express passenger locomotive for the line. As an 'import', with the implicit criticism of former policy that that entailed, he must have been particularly aware of the need to 'get it right' from the off. A year and half from taking office the first such engine, a Pacific, emerged. It had four cylinders ('because he was used

to it', says Bulleid) and was in many ways the logical progression, in dimension and form, from a 4-6-0. Three of the new Pacifics had been ordered under the 1933 Building Programme; these were the Princess Royal class and thirteen were built in all, in two batches, between the 1933 and 1935 Building Programmes, from 6200 appearing in July 1933 to 6212 in October 1935.

Onward and Upward
More of these elegant Princess Royal Pacifics were to be built but despite the paralysing Slump (though ended in 1933, it still spread its shadow over much of Britain) this had become the decade of speed and sophistication. Something bigger and better was on the stocks but the process of change, from the Princess Royals to the Coronation Pacifics, goes curiously unheralded in the

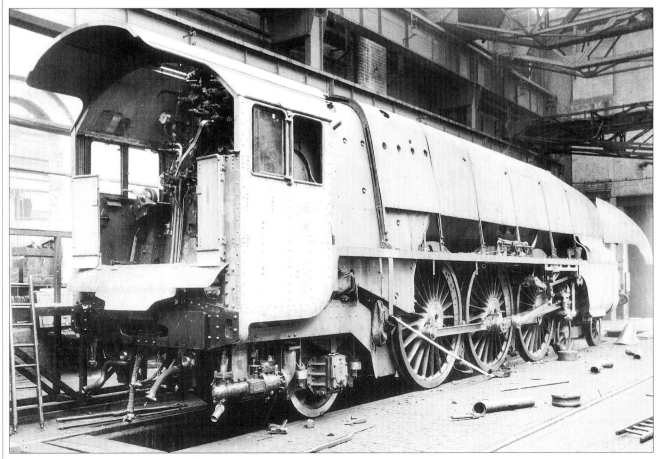

6220 under construction at Crewe in 1937. It affords a good view, for once, of the Davies & Metcalfe exhaust steam injector, prominent beneath the Fireman's side of the cab. Photograph National Railway Museum.

6220 is wheeled into the light for one of those comparisons beloved of the Publicity Department. The comparator is LION, and in a few weeks' time the two would be filmed together on the North Wales main line, for yet further publicity machinations. Photograph National Railway Museum.

LMS Minutes. The 1937 Building Programme listed 4F 0-6-0s, 3P 2-6-2Ts and diesel shunters, and was agreed on 26 July 1936. Normally such proposals went forward to the Board for 'rubber-stamping'. Now, the first five Coronation Pacifics, 6220-6224, were built in 1937 but authority only seems to have been given at a late stage, *after* the 1937 Programme got to the Board. Five more *Princesses* had been envisaged, but memories of West Coast - East Coast speed

rivalry were being thoroughly stirred and a series of high speed tests conducted during 1936 proved that better timings on the West Coast were perfectly possible. A degree of secrecy, or at least discretion, was obviously thought prudent. Gresley's three week-old SILVER LINK had reached 112½mph (twice within ten minutes!) in September 1935, and SILVER FOX 113mph in 1936. The LMS effort was now only a matter of time, and the means to do it would be a class of 'improved Princesses'.

1937: 6220-6224
The first of the new engines, more precisely (and awkwardly - it didn't catch on) called the 'Princess (Coronation) class', came out of Crewe with a 'date built' of 1 June 1937. This was 6220 CORONATION. The first batch, of five, in 1937, was as follows:
6220 CORONATION
6221 QUEEN ELIZABETH
6222 QUEEN MARY
6223 PRINCESS ALICE
6224 PRINCESS ALEXANDRA

6244 KING GEORGE VI, photographed for the record - note the full cowl at the front of the tender top. Now, it is never absolutely clear what we are looking at with these LMS photographs, because of the company's naughty habit of swopping identities rather than go through the tiresome process of wheeling in the right locomotive, or even waiting for to be built! See page 18 for one of the fakes. This one seems to be real; turned out in red as CITY OF LEEDS, it was renamed in honour of the King in April 1941, presumably for reasons of morale. Photograph National Railway Museum.

You'll Remember those Black and White Days...

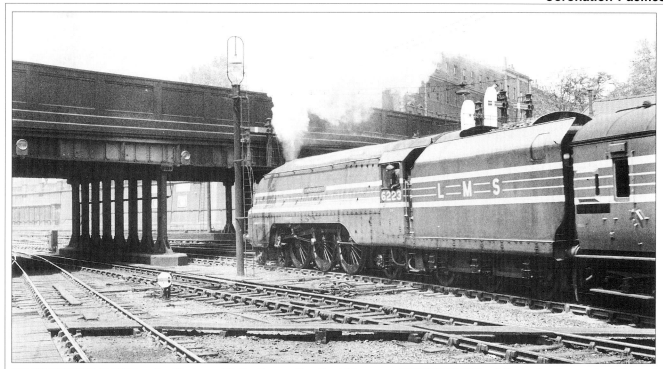

6223 PRINCESS ALICE leaving Euston with the Coronation Scot. The name CORONATION (and the train of course) celebrated King George VI's Coronation of 1937 and the other four of that 1937 batch continued the theme, as it were. They were all named after the immediate Royal Family—the Queen, the Queen Mother—and two Princesses who had not had a Princess Royal Pacific named after them.

The new Pacifics were very different indeed from the earlier Princesses and something of the way in which they came into being is revealed in the name. An almost covert period of design and construction hid from general view the way the existing Princess design was expanded beyond recognition. Hence the first (amended) official title, which certainly *looked* like an afterthought. A surprising aspect is that Stanier was away for much of the design period; he served in India on the Pacific Locomotive Investigation Committee, leaving it in the hands of assistants, principally Coleman, Riddles and Bond. The boiler was bigger and better, with more superheat, greatly increased firebox and total heating surface, bigger driving wheels (from 6ft.6in. to 6ft.9in.) and a greater diameter boiler at the firebox end. There were four cylinders again, but an arrangement of rocking levers (the work of Coleman) drove the inside valves from the outside motion. This gave the Coronations two sets of valve gear instead of four. Through this arrangement the outside cylinders could be positioned in a more conventional and satisfying way, between the bogie wheels. (On the preceding Princess Royals they were sited over the trailing bogie wheel.) The disposition had an added advantage, in that the leading flange of the outside cylinders overlapped the rear flange of the inside cylinder casting, imparting great rigidity where such multi-cylinder locomotives had traditionally been prone to weakness. As well as saving weight, getting rid of so much inside gear saved a constant labour of oiling and maintenance. There was a general imperative to lose weight as the design expanded to the very limits of loading and gauge, utilising the latest available materials and techniques. It was a process made possible by advances in materials— better, stronger, lighter alloy steels for boiler and frame and so on—just such a procedure was repeated again with the Britannias and 9Fs under

Exquisitely shining 6227 DUCHESS OF DEVONSHIRE at Crewe about 1938; an unusual view, the engine has charge of a single coach, with a 3F 0-6-0T at the other end. The explanation is that the coach is a GWR through vehicle to Scotland, collected by the South pilot and propelled onto 6227 waiting to take over a Euston - Scotland train. The coach would be on the front going north and on the rear coming back, ready for despatch to that strange country ruled by the GWR, while the Euston express hurried south.

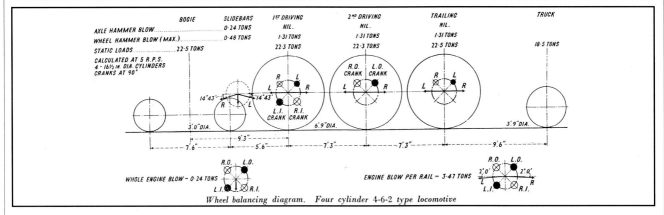

Wheel balancing diagram. Four cylinder 4-6-2 type locomotive

BR, with a still later generation of materials.

The weight problem was probably brought to particular prominence at the design stage of the Coronations because the engines had streamlining, with all its attendant inconveniences and its 'dead' weight. Yet CORONATION, a high speed machine and the first streamlined locomotive for the LMS, incorporated no fundamental break from conventional practice, in the sense of the materials used in its construction. *The Railway Gazette*, 'by the courtesy of the company's Chief Mechanical Engineer, Mr. W.A. Stanier' was given access to 'sources and data regarding the problems that arose'. It was, above all, *reliability* that Stanier was after: *'The Coronation locomotive (is) not actually one in which any very great departure has been made from current practice, so far as the materials of construction are concerned. In instituting so important a service as the Coronation Scot train, the first and essential requisite of the locomotive was that already referred to—namely, complete reliability. For this reason, previously untried and experimental materials were not used, and no material has been built into the engine which has not already been incorporated in some form or other on other modern locomotives of the LMSR. From the purely metallurgical point of view, therefore, the engine may be said to embody all that is of true worth in the best modern practice. On the other hand, the design of so powerful an engine within the allowable axle weights was not accomplished without very particular thought being given to the metallurgical side, even within the limitations outlined...'*

Valve events were 'smoothed out' in line with the best practice then permeating British design from France, emanating from the work of Chapelon. In this respect the Coronations represented a distinct progression beyond the earlier Princess Royal Pacifics. It was the larger piston valves and streamlined steam and exhaust passages that made them so free running. This, if you like, was Coleman's greatest contribution.

These were the real technical advances, but what is more important, after all, is that the design was a success right from the off - spectacularly so. 6220 ran a special for the gentlemen of the press on 29 June 1937 to demonstrate what was possible between Euston and Crewe. This led to the celebrated braking incident just south of Crewe. 6220 touched 114mph (some made it 113mph, only the equal of the LNER record) and but for the limited distance available for braking it would have been more conclusive. Rowledge mentions the unfortunate effect on the crockery and Bulleid refers to Lemon bracing his feet on the opposite seat in anticipation of the inevitable derailment.

From this time on, though they were overshadowed by the speedier activities to the east, the Coronation Pacifics established (in the eyes of many) their station as the most powerful and impressive of all the British Pacifics. There are many technical arguments as to which class brought engineering innovation, combined with subtlety

Born into dull black for 6248, to traffic in October 1943 and bearing the name first carried by 6244—see page 4. An excellent view of the hollowed out axles. In the midst of darkness, this was nonetheless the eleventh streamlined Pacific of the War—*Kreigslokomotiv* it wasn't.

6235 CITY OF BIRMINGHAM, the first of the City series, after 'de-streamlining'; an official record presumably taken in 1946, when the casing was removed. 6235 was one of three with crests, or rather coats of arms, placed above the nameplate. 6240 and 6254 were the others, and CORONATION itself had a crown. The curious notch in the boiler cladding had no other purpose than to provide room for the mechanical lubricator lids to be lifted clear. Photograph National Railway Museum.

of thought and brilliance of design, together with success on the road to a pinnacle of achievement in this country, but that in a sense is a redundant art. Few now even have the rudiments of steam locomotive design and the men responsible for the Pacifics of the 1930s and those who honed such machines through to the 1950s were towering figures in their field. Stanier, after all, was made a Fellow of the Royal Society. Our appreciation now, as regards the steam locomotive, is largely a matter of sentiment and who is to say now which class might have been 'the best'. Was a Britannia a better piece of engineering? Or a rebuilt Merchant Navy? And if they were, so they should be, building as they did on the earlier work of masters.

Ah, but then, but then... As one raised from the first on East Coast Pacifics, I can attest to the sheer eye-popping majesty of these vast things, when first visited upon the impressionable mind. Somehow, no other locomotives in Britain contrived to expand and flow outwards to fill the loading gauge, and somehow dwarf anything around them. Thus the Crewe term the 'Big 'Uns' (which seems to have used nowhere else—see Baker's *Crewe Sheds*) was justly earned.

That Streamlining
It was the engineering which made the 'Improved Princesses' such a success, not the streamlining, which we can now see to have had little more efficacy that the 'go-faster' airfoil on a family car. The LMS streamlining suffered aesthetically too (at least it seems that way to us now), though this might have a deal to do with having 'come second' in the speed stakes. The LNER had got

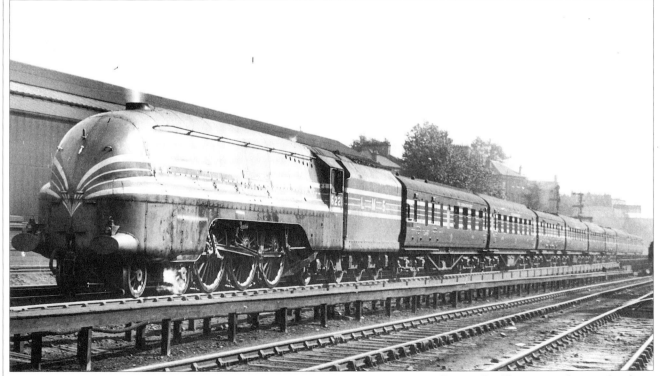

6221 QUEEN ELIZABETH, leaving London with the Coronation Scot about 1937-38. The new Pacifics were at the very forefront of design: as Stanier's notes to *The Railway Gazette* put it, the brief was to increase the power and reliability of the earlier Princess Royal class while restricting, so far as was possible, any increase in weight, *'...so designing and constructing the engine that in spite of the considerable and sustained demands made upon it, it should at all times be equal to the task and able therefore, to maintain the reputation of the service in respect of speed and punctuality'*. Which, mostly, is what they did.

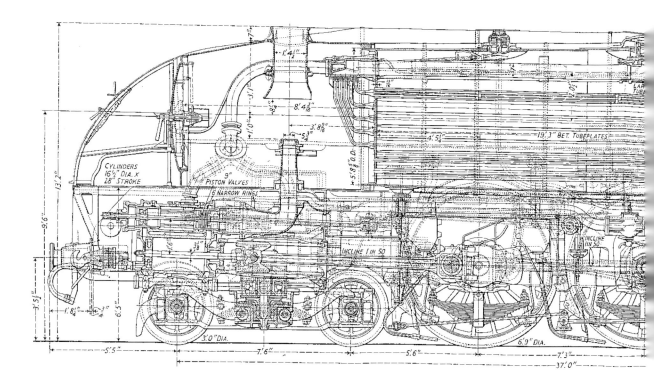

And how they ended up. That unforgettable front end. Photograph J.G. Walmsley, B.P. Hoper Collection.

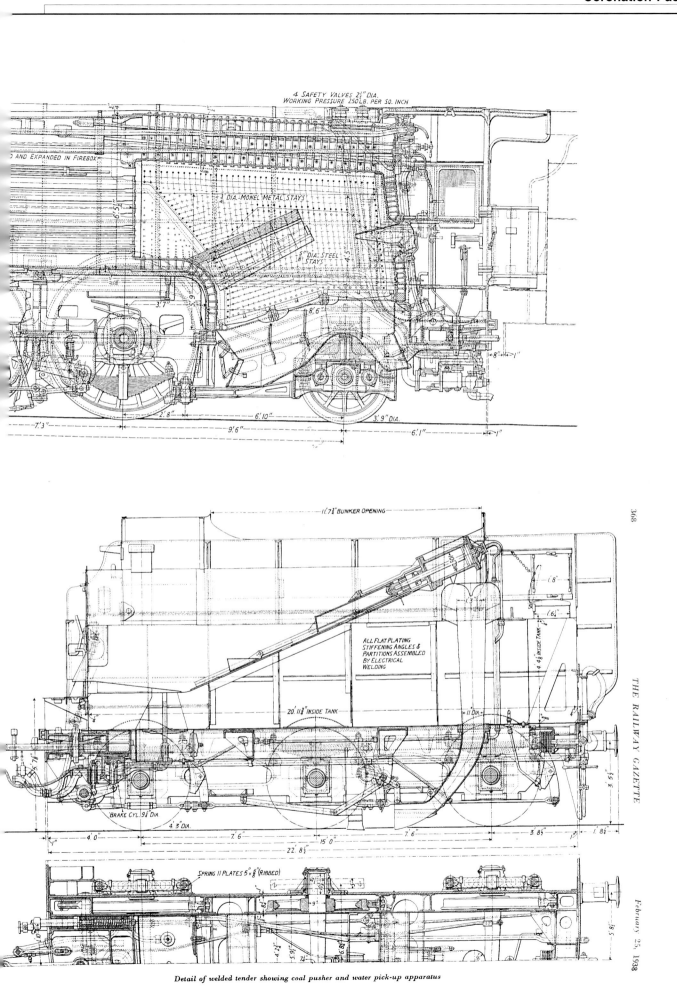

4 SAFETY VALVES 2½" DIA.
WORKING PRESSURE 250 LB. PER SQ. INCH

AND EXPANDED IN FIREBOX

⅞ DIA. MONEL METAL STAYS

⅞ DIA. STEEL STAYS

11'.7¾" BUNKER OPENING

ALL FLAT PLATING
STIFFENING ANGLES &
PARTITIONS ASSEMBLED
BY ELECTRICAL
WELDING

4'.4⅝" INSIDE TANK

20'.11¾" INSIDE TANK

11 DIA.

BRAKE CYL. 9¼" DIA.

4'.3" DIA.

SPRING 11 PLATES 5" × ⅝" (RIBBED)

368

THE RAILWAY GAZETTE

February 25, 1938

Detail of welded tender showing coal pusher and water pick-up apparatus

6227 DUCHESS OF DEVONSHIRE in red livery at Polmadie, 1938. The provision of the streamlined case and, especially, its *continued* provision, is all the more remarkable given that weight reduction was so vital in the design of 'the big 'uns'. Despite the casing, more than five tons had been saved; the locomotives were up to the very limit allowed by the LMS Civil Engineer and without the saving *'a very considerable reduction in the size of the boiler and capacity of the engine would have been necessary'*.

there first of course, in all senses and while to many the streamlining sits well on the A4—perfectly is probably a better word—the Stanier version has a rather unfortunate 'bulbosity'. But this, again, is in the mind; the fact is, far less people actually *remember*, now, the LMS streamlining and it no longer exists for a new generation to admire. Moreover, the original A4 streamlining was improved no end by the removal (for chance reasons, really) of those unfortunate 'skirts', which so reduced the classic rakish look of the locos.

It is generally agreed that the LMS streamlining was for publicity reasons and nothing else, whatever technical arguments might have been advanced. Without the PR people 'inquiring as to what might be done' Stanier would hardly have given it a thought. The new engines would power a new high speed train, the Coronation Scot from Euston to Glasgow and streamlining, for the locomotive at least, was *de rigueur*. The fact of streamlining mattered hardly a jot, but it would just have to be used, in keeping with the current public mood. Bulleid in his *Master Builders of Steam* describes a scene in which Coleman ('one of us' in the new order, and highly effective Chief Draughtsman; a Horwich man in charge of both Derby and Crewe!) comes up with a suitable form of casing and the drawings duly go off to Crewe. Vice President Hartley, anxious to be thoroughly up

to date, urges Stanier to conduct wind tunnel tests to determine the best shape. This is carried out and Coleman's shape (already 'done and dusted' and being proceeded with at Crewe) inevitably turns out to be the best. The famous Lady Godiva story dates from this time; doubts about the suitability of the streamlining filtered down from the Board and Coleman drew a conventional version, duly named Lady Godiva. The streamlining went ahead.

1938: 6225-6234
New 'Princess (Coronation)' engines were soon on the way and it was not long before the more sensible term 'Coronation' was in use. This is a Mechanical and Electrical Engineering Committee Minute of 27 October 1937:

'Locomotive Programme 1938. Construction of ten additional Passenger Engines and retention in service of engines previously authorised for displacement. Submitted memorandum (October 1937) from the Chief Operating Manager and Chief Mechanical Engineer, recommending that to meet increased demands in engine power due to the increase in volume of traffic, ten additional Class 7 4-6-2 express passenger tender locomotives (Coronation type) be provided at a total approximate outlay of £138,000, the expenditure to be dealt with in conjunction with the 1938 Rolling

Stock Building Programme and reported on completion of that Programme. It was also recommended that certain locomotives already approved for breaking up should be retained, where retention would be possible without the necessity of building new boilers, the actual retentions being reported in due course and reviewed periodically.

'The Executive Committee had approved the proposal and with the Chairman's authority arrangements had been made, in anticipation of the approval of the Directors, for the necessary material for the proposed ten new engines to be ordered.

'To permit of the Class 7 engines running between Crewe and Manchester, and Holyhead, it was proposed to reconstruct Bridge No.90 between Handford and Cheadle Hulme, over which there was at present a speed restriction, and a separate recommendation would be made in due course to the Works Committee. The bridges at Llanfairfechan and Queensferry on the line between Chester and Holyhead, which were also restricted, were now being reconstructed.

'Approved, so far as the Mechanical and Electrical Engineering Committee was concerned.'

The ten the LMS got for its £138,000 were the 'Duchesses' (by which name most of us habitually called all of them in the 1950s and 1960s), as follows:

6225 DUCHESS OF GLOUCESTER

6226 DUCHESS OF NORFOLK

6227 DUCHESS OF DEVONSHIRE

6228 DUCHESS OF RUTLAND

6229 DUCHESS OF HAMILTON
All Streamlined

6230 DUCHESS OF BUCCLEUCH

6231 DUCHESS OF ATHOLL

6232 DUCHESS OF MONTROSE

6233 DUCHESS OF SUTHERLAND

6234 DUCHESS OF ABERCORN
All Non-streamlined

They appeared between May and September and the crucial change was that some, 6230-6234, were built without the streamlined casing, but without smoke deflectors. (The problem of smoke blowing down and obscuring drivers' vision was yet to manifest itself. Double chimneys, as they were fitted were probably also a factor, as with the Gresley A3s.) Essery and Jenkinson (*An Illustrated History of LMS Locomotives*, Silver Link, 1989) recount a story of Riddles' at the time; Stanier apparently made little secret of his scepticism regarding streamlining and simply determined to build 'five proper ones too'.

'...a little over 2%'

Now that there were engines in both streamlined and conventional form, comparisons were inevitably there to be made. Did it make any difference for a start? The Engineering Section of the Research Department at Derby issued a *Memorandum* on 25 October 1938, detailing coal consumption between the streamlined and non-streamlined 1938 engines, 6225-6228 and 6230-6334 respectively. (6229 was still under construction while the comparisons were being made.) All the engines were put on Camden jobs, including the Coronation Scot, for the sake of the comparison. Coal consumption figures for the eight week period had not showed the streamlined engines in a particularly favourable light; Derby nevertheless provided wind tunnel results that showed it did. These 'proved', on computation of 'still air' conditions, a given coal consumption figure, mileages and average speeds, that a 'predicted saving' in coal was inevitable. For the more everyday Camden jobs, this saving varied from 7.72 to 12.79 tons per four week period, and for the Coronation Scot, 11.82 tons every four weeks - near-enough 150 tons a year over a non-streamlined engine.

Results obtained the traditional way had indicated the *opposite*, but Derby had the answers. The coaling plant records were notoriously inaccurate, it was declared, while the error due to spillage was compounded in the case of the streamlined engines by the shape of the tenders: *'The error due to spillage during the coaling operation is more serious with streamlined locomotives than with others, leading to an apparent coal consumption greater than the actual. The cover over the front end of the tender of the streamlined locomotives directly spills any coal which accidentally falls on it, and such spillage may be appreciable since the engine crew try to fill the tender as far forward as possible. At best some empty space under the cover remains, and in the endeavour to compensate for it, coal is piled as high as permissible over the rest of the tender bunker which leads, it is said, to a proportion of spillage that is especially marked with streamlined engines.'*

Derby protested that consumption figures used to show that there was in fact *no* difference between conventional and streamlined engines were not properly obtained, in that they were not comparing like with like. The streamlined engines covered less miles and the coal consumption figures were given for five non-streamlined engines, while only four (6229 was missing remember) were on trial. Consumption varied (questions had been asked in high places and they didn't come much higher than the Chief Operating Manager and the Chief Accountant) with the same locomotive on different

The Coronation Scot at Berkhamsted, 11 July 1939. It is difficult now to appreciate the sense of wonder associated with all the streamlining extravagances of the 1930s. The PR boys knew they were tapping a vast well of interest in such matters, among the general public as much as the enthusiasts. Families broke their journeys, office workers tarried, schoolboys skipped lessons, just to say they had glimpsed such marvels. Photograph H.C. Casserley.

6221 QUEEN ELIZABETH in its blue livery at Edinburgh Princes Street in 1937. Pre-war, the LMS competed with the LNER for the Edinburgh-Glasgow business, even though its route via Shotts was more difficult. By 1939 there was one train, the 1.30pm Glasgow Central to Edinburgh Princes Street, that did the run in 61 minutes non-stop. The trains had Restaurant Cars and the most powerful locomotives were employed—for the Coronations these were daytime fill in turns, and this practice continued after the War's end. The 'streamlined' lamps are worth a chuckle; the curious 'flag' on the top lamp bracket is a purely Scottish device dating from Caledonian days—the correct Caley term was 'semaphore route indicator'. It indicated the route to be followed, which in the context of Edinburgh would denote Glasgow or Carlisle. They could even be seen on Britannia and Clan Pacifics, well into the 1950s. Photograph P. Ransome Wallis.

jobs, and between different locomotives of the same group on the same job far beyond that attributable to streamlining, for any number of reasons. The steam locomotive was just *like* that, and 6227 and 6228 for instance, showed a difference of over 14% on some jobs and nearly 23% on others, depending on driver, weather, steaming and any number of other foibles. The interesting figure, that Derby was convinced of, was that, with all these factors stripped away, streamlining gave a coal consumption advantage of 'a little over 2%'. At this, Stanier probably smiled a bit.

No.6225, new on 11 May 1938, ran a special train between Euston and Glasgow on 8 June, in connection with a meeting of the Institution of Locomotive Engineers held in Glasgow. It was proposed to put on something of a show for visiting officials of the German State Railways (Germany had earlier loomed large in the speed contests, with 124½mph (200.4kph) in 1935, with Borsig 4-6-4 05.001) and the special left Euston with these guests and the members of the Institution. The dynamometer car was attached 'in order that observations could be made by the party en route, and that a complete dynamometer car test could be made.'

DUCHESS OF GLOUCESTER had run 3,502 miles since new and steamed throughout 'very satisfactorily'. A schedule of 6 hours 55 minutes gave an average speed of 58.5mph while the actual average was 59.2mph. Steaming was very free, with full boiler pressure maintained 'without difficulty'. Maximum drawbar horsepower registered between Tebay and Shap was 830, and between Beattock and Beattock Summit 1,153. Maximum speed was 88mph approaching Euxton Junction, south of Preston. Train weight was only 232 tons but the outing made the show it was meant to. The LMS Report concluded *'In consideration of the total weight of the engine and train, and the high average speed, the results obtained, both on the Drawbar Horse Power basis and in general, indicate exceptional economy'*. The truly spectacular feats of haulage were to come the following year, heralding what was to come in the War - and there certainly wouldn't be any more German passengers for a while...

6234 and double chimneys

Nevertheless, in the inauspicious year of 1939 a truly awe-inspiring feat demonstrated just what a Coronation could do. Whether in any way it anticipated the sort of work the locos would indeed be called upon to do in the Second World War is not known - probably not, because they were put into store at 'safe'

places on the outbreak of hostilities, only to be brought back after a few weeks when someone realised how daft it was. Rowledge in *The LMS Pacifics* and Allen before him, in *British Pacific Locomotives*) describes how 6234 DUCHESS OF ABERCORN, newly modified with double blastpipe and chimney, took twenty coaches (a little over 600 tons) from Crewe to Glasgow on 26 February 1939, returning to Crewe after a couple of hours, with no special attention at Polmadie in the meantime. It was designed to emulate a run in normal service, and the train began the return from Glasgow after just two hours. The trip was full of superlatives, particularly 6234's effort in taking the train, more than twice the load of the Coronation Scot, from Glasgow to Carlisle in only 90 seconds over the schedule of that prestigious train. It was glory-and-trumpets stuff, with an unprecedented maximum drawbar horsepower of 2,511 southbound from Carlisle (with Crewe men).

DUCHESS OF ABERCORN had been tested only a fortnight before in its single chimney state, with the same load, and the performance had been lack-lustre by comparison. It had proved impossible to keep time or full steam pressure; the contrast was so dramatic that double blastpipes were immediately seen as a most desirable modification. The 1939 engines (and all subsequently) accordingly emerged new with the double chimney. All the existing single chimney engines were converted as soon as maybe - all were done before the end of the War.

1939: 6235-6239

This conventional batch of 1938, 6230-6234, was doubtless the way Stanier would have liked the rest to appear, but once streamlining had taken such a hold it was difficult to shake it off - the 2% figure seems to have 'stuck'. Bulleid in his *Master Builders of Steam* does not mention the streamlining business discussed above but does give a short account of the Research Department and Stanier's relations with it. The Research people were 'inclined to become theoretical' he says, and Stanier found it 'distant and ponderous'. They had a shorter, easier, line of access to the Vice President and Stanier 'got slightly cross...'

The 1939 Building Programme was approved on 27 July 1938 and gave authority for twenty further Coronations, described as '7P Pacifics' at a cost of £243,000. The earlier batch of ten, 6225-6234, as we've seen above, was still under construction but, it was noted, there was still plenty of work for such engines, 'having regard to the weight of the express passenger trains on which it is proposed to use them, and the speeds at which they are timed'.

The twenty approved in July 1938 were the 'City' ones; as long ago as 1928 Fowler had reported that building new locomotives in the same year in which they were authorised

had become impossible and by 1939 other factors were beginning to bear. The country had already avoided what seemed like certain war in 1938 but in the summer of 1939 it was finally apparent to all who could see that it would, indeed, come. Plans were made even back in 1938 (as touched upon above) to put big express locomotives into store when war came, in the belief that no 'ordinary' passenger trains would be run. These plans were dusted off in the summer of 1939, so it was hardly surprising that production of Coronations at Crewe should falter somewhat. In the event only five, all streamlined, came out in 1939:

6235 CITY OF BIRMINGHAM
6236 CITY OF BRADFORD
6237 CITY OF BRISTOL
6238 CITY OF CARLISLE
6239 CITY OF CHESTER

1940: 6240-6244

The Building Programme for 1940, promulgated on 28 June 1939, foresaw no Pacifics. The programme of twenty streamlined engines approved in 1938 was well behind and only five more came out in 1940, all streamlined. These appeared between March and July and it is perhaps surprising that streamlining was retained. The magic figure of 2% saving in coal, perhaps, still held sway over increased awkwardness of servicing and repair. The LNER, remember, took the A4s' sideskirts off pretty quick, and they never returned. Indeed, few engines could look more sorry for themselves than a streamlined Coronation at the War's end, unkempt and tired. It was the same with the A4s, for streamlining suffered

disproportionately in the face of neglect. The five streamlined Coronations produced in 1940 were:

6240 CITY OF COVENTRY
6241 CITY OF EDINBURGH
6242 CITY OF GLASGOW
6243 CITY OF LANCASTER
6244 CITY OF LEEDS (renamed KING GEORGE VI April 1941)

The LMS *War Report* (published after the War but still labelled 'secret') made these comments: '*The succession of air raid warnings during the autumn - winter months of 1940, coupled with the restrictive effect of black-out conditions, had increased the difficulties of the engine power position, and in a review prepared for submission to the Minister of War Transport on the locomotive position on the railways during 1940, reference was made to the serious over-taxing of freight engines. On account of the shortage of materials, the locomotive building programmes had not come up to expectations; the actual building completed during the year was described as "trifling". The LMS deliveries of new engines had not exceeded 24, making a total output from the Company's shops of 40 engines since the beginning of the war.*'

1943: 6245-6248

The Second World War thoroughly interrupted and upset the Pacific programme on the LMS and came close to choking it off altogether. Had not War broken out doubtless more would have been built and there would not have been such a curiously low total of Pacifics on the West Coast. Assuredly, too, the

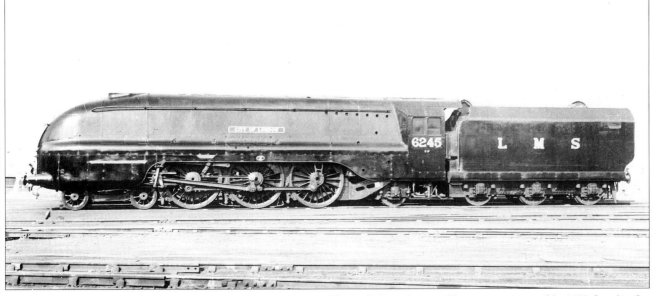

6245 CITY OF LONDON, new in its wartime black, June 1943. The building of streamliners was resumed in 1939 despite the international situation and the acknowledged difficulties of the streamline case when it came to routine maintenance. And despite the fact that, in any event, it was planned that the big express engines would be promptly mothballed on the outbreak of hostilities anyway! Construction, apparently, proceeded on the orders of Lord Stamp, the LMS President; in the event such engines (on the LNER too) proved invaluable in the War in heaving packed trains of almost unimaginable length between London and Scotland. Photograph National Railway Museum.

planned bigger versions would have come to fruition. A Minute of the Mechanical and Electrical Engineering Committee of 24 April 1941 describes the position: 'The locomotives authorised under the 1939 and 1940 Locomotive Renewal Programmes and the Special Programme authorised by Board Minute had not yet been constructed and ... the Chief Mechanical Engineer anticipated 208 locomotives would be completed prior to 31st December 1942 leaving 108 locomotives to be built in 1943 to complete existing authorised programmes. To be built prior to 31st December 1942:

6222 QUEEN MARY striking a classic pose with the Coronation Scot train over Shap, about 1938.

Class 8 2-8-0 freight tender	93
Class 5 4-6-0 mixed traffic tender	35
0-6-0 diesel electric shunting	59
Class 4 2-6-4 passenger tank	13
Class 7 4-6-2 passenger tender	8

To be built during 1943:

0-6-0 diesel electrical shunting	61
Class 4 2-6-4 passenger tank	45
Class 7 4-6-2 passenger tender	2'

These last two were to have 'experimental features' which included a boiler pressure of 300lb/sq.in., more superheat and other improvements. This was not really feasible in wartime but would at last see completion of the batch of twenty approved way back in 1938 - but no. The report continues: 'Having regard to the necessity for continuity of production, entailing the ordering of material well in advance, it was considered inadvisable to cancel the authority already obtained for building engines which would be delivered by the end of 1942, nor would it be advisable to cancel the authority for the 0-6-0 diesel electric shunting engines in view of the fact that the chassis only were being built in the company's workshop and the diesel engines and electrical equipment were obtained from outside contractors.

'It was however recommended that the authority for building the 45 class 4 2-6-4 passenger tank engines and the 2 class 7 4-6-2 passenger tender engines be cancelled and a new programme be put forward for 1943 when the position could be reconsidered in the light of the circumstances then prevailing.'

As it turned out, no new Pacifics would come until 1943, and then only four, and streamlined to boot! One, 6248, would keep its casing barely *three* years:

6245 CITY OF LONDON
6246 CITY OF MANCHESTER
6247 CITY OF LIVERPOOL
6248 CITY OF LEEDS

'The position for locomotives had become much more favourable during 1943, and reached a higher level than at any time since the outbreak of the war' declares the LMS *War Report*. The improvement was due to the loan of American and WD engines and the fact that no more engines had to be released for Government use. The four streamlined Pacifics built in 1943, as we have seen, were long overdue from the 1939 Programme, approved in 1938. Along with twenty Class Fives and a pair of

The famous 'gape' of a Coronation, rather less dramatic than that of an A4 and, it is suspected, rather more awkward to use on some crowded shed roads. Photograph National Railway Museum.

2-6-4Ts from the same programme and a hundred or more 8Fs from the 1940 and 1943 Programmes, these were described as 'Supplementations to the Locomotive Stock'.

1944: 6249-6252
Four more Coronations in 1944 saw the 1939 Programme of twenty nearly complete:

6249 CITY OF SHEFFIELD
6250 CITY OF LICHFIELD
6251 CITY OF NOTTINGHAM
6252 CITY OF LEICESTER

Light was dawning; these were *not* streamlined, and brought to eighteen the engines approved way back in 1938. Two thus remained to be built of that 1939 Programme but these got lost somehow - presumably the two that were to have 'experimental features' were regarded separately. So, by the end of 1944 thirty-three had been built, albeit at an agonisingly slow pace. Few other major classes could have been built in so many batches, of so few locos each. This was all due to the War of course but there was to be no surge of building after 1945. In 1944 five more Coronations were recommended and these would be the last. They were detailed to the Mechanical and Electrical Engineering Committee on 23 November 1944 and it is an indication of how far adrift construction had got that it referred to requirements two years' hence, in 1946:
Locomotive Renewal Programme 1946
Recommend 105 new engines, £905,600; includes five Class 7 4-6-2 passenger tender (non streamlined)

£75,850. Total includes ten each of new design of 2-6-2 Passenger Tank and 2-6-0 Freight Tender.

1946-48: 6253-6257
The last five engines (all non-streamlined of course) were:

6253 CITY OF ST ALBANS
6254 CITY OF STOKE-ON-TRENT
6255 CITY OF HEREFORD
6256 SIR WILLIAM A. STANIER, F.R.S.
6257 CITY OF SALFORD

The first three came out in September and October 1946 but there was a pause for the last two. These were different in a way rather beyond the endless differences which had appeared in the class. These were 'deliberate' and were meant to bring together all the various improvements which more than ten years of experience had thrown up, as well as latest ideas of design, materials and construction. In a sort of carry over from the two which were to have 'experimental features', the last two Coronations were built at the same time as the LMS main line diesels; Ivatt was now in charge but he announced his belief that the *'conventional reciprocating steam locomotive is still capable of considerable advance and that the ceiling of operating availability and maintenance cost per mile had not yet been reached'*. Of this, more anon...

***

The last two came out in 1947 and 1948 respectively. The intention was to incorporate all the detail improvements to rectify the problems thrown up during the long, hard and drastically changed conditions that had been seen since the first engine had been introduced in 1937 - more

than ten years to bring a class of 38 into service! Roller bearings throughout and manganese steel linings to the axleboxes and hornguides were fitted, to raise the mileages between shoppings to an annual magic figure (never realised) of 100,000. The visual differences were fairly marked, and principally concerned the cast steel Delta trailing truck, redesigned after some false starts to make room for the new innovation of a rocking grate, together with hopper ashpan, again redesigned to suit. 46257, the last, was always a notorious rough rider, and remained so throughout its career. The trailing truck was closely based on the American S160 2-8-0s which had worked in Britain during the War. The truck did not perform as expected and much time was taken up during this period with modifications and alterations. Another alteration consequent upon these rear end changes was the different cab sheets found in 46256 and 46257. This is said to have imparted a passing resemblance to the WD 2-8-0s(!), and in some quarters (definitely *not* Crewe North) this was said to have made for the nickname 'Austerity 4-6-2s'

The new reverser (used afterwards for the new BR Standards) was a prominent alteration but other visual manifestations on the last two, the crowning glories of the class, were very small. The design had been honed and upgraded after being tempered in the fire of war, so that, at the dawn of BR, they were the very acme of British Pacific design. The stage was surely set for further production but: that was it. There is, however, much more to the story...

6221 QUEEN ELIZABETH roped off for viewing at Glasgow Central in 1937. The blue ones always stood out a little, in the enthusiast mind at least, for though the other Coronations were red, so were all the other LMS express types.

6222 QUEEN MARY uncovered; to many, the very acme of the steam locomotive, unparalleled in its combination of power and grace, swelling and flowing almost to fill every available inch of the loading gauge. The unfortunate slope of the smokebox was eventually rectified in all the engines of course, though it did provide us with a typically understated British nickname, 'Semi'. This feature remains curiously popular among some die-hards, especially those who knew them at the time, though to any who came late to the class, when most had a conventional smokebox, 'that slope' always appeared as a sort of deficiency. Note small cab window and smoke deflectors; a small space to match the handholds was soon cut at the base, to give more room for a cleaner's toe cap. Though it is not readily apparent, the footplate tapered to almost nothing at this point, which was obviously the cause of the problem — the cleaner ran out of room! The engine is at Camden, ready to back down to Euston; hence the over-full tender. Photograph P. Ransome Wallis.

SOME CHANGES AND DIFFERENCES

*'the engines have proved highly successful, and the percentage of punctual
arrivals at each end has been uniformly high'*

6224 PRINCESS ALEXANDRA, leaving Crewe with ordinary stock, with through GW coaches at the front. The brilliant blue livery had to be cleaned according to a rigorous regime and just the ordinary stains of starting away could spoil the overall effect—witness the dirty water streaks down the side of the casing. The horizontal stripes rapidly lost their 'speed' effect when marred like this. Out on the road, there was little that could be done about it but the job must have caused staffing problems at Camden, where all the streamliners first went. Photograph P. Ransome Wallis.

There are probably few classes which provide more fertile ground for the 'engine picker'— that devotee of detail—than the Coronation Pacifics. This account attempts to chart some of these, as well as drawing attention to many in the relevant captions. Most such features are well known but others less so, and one or two aspects are shown, it is felt, that do not seem to have got much attention previously. At the same time, a prudent man shrinks from any claim to a wholly definitive guide to detail differences among the Coronations. One of the pleasures of 'engine picking' is that such a complete condition, in which the pen can be put down and the pronouncement made, *'that is the tale complete'*, almost certainly does not exist. Always, one more photograph will turn up, revealing some unsuspected trifle...

The class could not have enjoyed any difference more fundamental than that—uniquely in British practice—it was divided into streamlined and non-streamlined forms, if you ignore half-hearted experiments with odd members of otherwise conventional classes. The extraordinarily long time taken to complete the (relatively small) class,

along with the decision to 'de-streamline', exaggerated the range of detail variation. Some engines were losing the streamlined casing before some of the later examples appeared new from Crewe! There was a period when some ran without smoke deflectors, while the 'de-streamlined' examples went about for a further time with that 'shaved off' smokebox, an oddity which came to so typify 'the semi'.

Clothed and Unclothed; Streamlining, Smokeboxes and Front Framing

Streamlining added three tons to the weight of a Coronation. That, really, was it, and little good can be said of it. So far as aesthetics went it is, really, a hard one to call, for inevitably it would be a case of applying the mores and tastes of today. It is, however, useful to make one point; to the modern eye (something already mentioned in the previous section), the appearance of the Gresley A4s benefits no end from the removal of the 'skirts'. It does this, if you think about it, by revealing *the wheels*, and all their sense of power and speed. In the Coronations, on the other hand, although the overall form was

probably less rakish, the wheels were boldly revealed from the start. Even so, however 'bulbous' and rather matronly the design might look to us now, certainly the Coronations were regarded as striking at the time. The Coronation Scot train, brought into service between Euston and Glasgow on 5 July 1937, was not itself streamlined and was but standard stock given new interiors and 'redecorated' in blue with white stripes; the schedule was nothing dramatic, given the powers of the new engines, but the necessary PR 'splash' was duly made. The accelerated schedules to Glasgow, with one stop at Carlisle, covered the 401½ miles in 6½ hours, an average speed of 62.6mph. In something akin to what we might now call 'electric blue' the first five, 6220-6224, made a very fine show of it, with horizontal white lines sweeping round the casing from that tremendous V at the front.

The streamlining case was borne by a framework of light steel (less weighty materials were sought for every facet of the locos) while at the front it was supported on a forward extension of what would have been the footplate. The casing of course could only be a hindrance

Fake! A streamliner of the 'City' series, 6252 CITY OF SALFORD never existed and this photographic 'record' became nonsensical. 6252, when eventually built, was non-streamlined CITY OF LEICESTER, and CITY OF SALFORD, in the end, turned out to be the very last Coronation, appearing in BR times and incorporating all the Ivatt modifications—it could hardly have been more different from the fake one shown here. Note the early Stone-Deuta speed recorder (later removed) on a bracket by the rear driving wheel. Photograph National Railway Museum.

to those who had to maintain the engines but shed staff simply 'got on with it' when it came to the inconveniences of the streamlining. The War, however, brought a small revolution in attitudes to maintenance, encouraged by a number of factors. First of all, there was a war on - things *should* be less labour intensive; secondly American locomotives had shown that labour saving features were perfectly feasible and thirdly (there were other, social factors at work) there were less and less staff prepared to do these jobs. With wartime neglect, moreover (and the prospects of a return to 1930s standards ever more bleak) the streamliners looked absolutely terrible. On 24 October 1945 the Mechanical and Electrical Engineering Committee heard from the 'Acting CME' (this was Ivatt): *'the streamlined casing in the Coronation class 4-6-2 passenger locomotives was a disadvantage both from the point of view of its maintenance and of the inaccessibility of the engine generally resulting in increased maintenance expenditure, and with*

6233 DUCHESS OF SUTHERLAND of the original 1938 non-streamlined, single chimney batch, at Shrewsbury before the War. Doubtless this is the form of the Coronations 'as Nature intended' (as well as Stanier).

You'll Remember those Black and White Days...

Pre-war glories, a blaze of red and blue, at Camden shed about 1938, arranged no doubt for the Publicity Department. The streamliner on the right cannot be identified but it is not one of the first five of 1937, for they did not have the little ventilating louvre in front of the left-hand cylinder (denoted by the rectangular pattern of rivets between the buffer and the cylinder casing). One of the original streamliners, 6224 PRINCESS ALEXANDRA, stands in the middle and is seen to lack this little 'extra', which seems to have been restricted to the left side only. The single chimney non-streamliner is 6230 DUCHESS OF BUCCLEUCH and the Jubilee on the far right, closest to the main line is 5559 BRITISH COLUMBIA. The Royal Scot (with the old style Royal Scot headboard) remains unidentified.

the concurrence of the Chief Operating Manager, recommended that the casing be removed from the 24 [6220-6229 and 6235-6248] engines and that side deflector plates be provided at an estimated cost of £5,527'.

Allen (British Pacific Locomotives, Ian Allan, 1962) gives a similar technical justification,

noting at the same time that 'from the publicity point of view a coal-begrimed streamline casing is worse than none at all'. The reduction in atmospheric resistance, if it really existed, only began to make itself felt at speeds in excess of 80mph and as the speed limit generally was down to 75mph, the streamlining was looking sillier and sillier.

6235 CITY OF BIRMINGHAM was the first streamliner to metamorphose, in April 1946, emerging from Crewe with a set of detail differences setting it apart from those Coronations built non-streamlined from the first. The most peculiar manifestation of course was the sloping smokebox top. The wartime air of economy was a long

Red single chimney non-streamliner 6231 DUCHESS OF ATHOLL, with a streamliner behind, at Shrewsbury.

6234 DUCHESS OF ABERCORN heads north past Camden shed in its single chimney days. It was the prodigious feats of this engine, newly fitted with double chimney in February 1939, which prompted the rapid conversion of the others to the double arrangement.

CORONATIONS - SOME DETAIL CHANGES

Loco	To traffic	S/C	DC	SD added	SB restored
46220	6/37	S	12/44	9/46	12/55
46221	6/37	S	11/40	5/46	9/52
46222	6/37	S	8/43	5/46	8/53
46223	7/37	S	11/41	8/46	8/55
46224	7/37	S	5/40	5/46	10/54
46225	5/38	S	6/43	2/47	1/55
46226	5/38	S	7/42	6/47	11/55
46227	6/38	S	12/40	2/47	5/53
46228	6/38	S	9/40	7/47	1/57
46229	9/38	S	4/43	11/47	2/57
46230	6/38	C	10/40	9/46	-
46231	6/38	C	6/40	9/46	-
46232	7/38	C	1/43	2/45	-
46233	7/38	C	3/41	9/46	-
46234	8/38	C	2/39	3/46	-
46235	7/39	S	New	4/46	7/52
46236	7/39	S	New	12/47	11/53
46237	8/39	S	New	1/47	5/56
46238	9/39	S	New	11/46	10/53
46239	9/39	S	New	6/47	2/57
46240	3/40	S	New	6/47	5/57
46241	4/40	S	New	1/47	2/58
46242	5/40	S	New	3/47	11/53
46243	6/40	S	New	5/49	11/58
46244	7/40	S	New	8/47	7/53
46245	6/43	S	New	8/47	12/57
46246	8/43	S	New	9/46	5/60
46247	9/43	S	New	5/47	5/58
46248	10/43	S	New	12/46	6/58
46249	4/44	C	New	11/46	-
46250	5/44	C	New	3/46	-
46251	6/44	C	New	8/46	-
46252	6/44	C	New	3/45	
46253	9/46	C	New	New	-
46254	9/46	C	New	New	-
46255	10/46	C	New	New	-
46256	12/47	C	New	New	-
46257	5/48	C	New	New	-

S = Streamliner
C = Conventional
SD = Smoke Deflector
SB = Smokebox
DC = Double Chimney

way from the heady PR exercises of the late 1930s but in terms of styling the LMS seems to have gone into reverse. Saving the cost of a new smokebox, the original, with its sloping top was retained, imparting a most unsettling effect. By 1952 some were getting new smokeboxes to the conventional pattern but the last was not done, incredibly, until 1960!

The other altered detail consequent on the 'unfrocking' was the more utilitarian front end. The curved plating in front of the cylinders was removed. This became a feature of the engines that were de-streamlined, and was incorporated on new engines from 6253 to 6257. The other engines built in conventional form from the first, 6230-6234 and 6249-6252 kept the footplate draped in front of the cylinders. 46242 was unusual; 'de-streamlined' in March 1947, it had been near-destroyed in the Harrow disaster of 1952. Emerging after reconstruction it was seen to have the old-style footplating, curving down in front of its cylinders.

The first smoke deflectors appeared on 6232 and 6252 in 1945 and the rest of the non-streamliners got them the following year. The streamlined engines were equipped with smoke deflectors when the casings were removed. The Record Cards often lack continuity of detail, which is part both of their fascination and their capacity to frustrate the Seekers After Truth. The fitting of

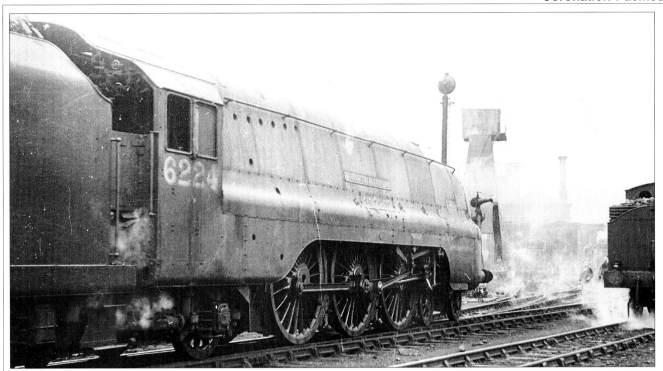

A sorry streamliner, 6224 PRINCESS ALEXANDRA at Camden 9 June 1945. The wartime black had been put on the previous October but such is the layer of grime it would probably not look much different even if the stripes were still there. In the drive to keep engines in traffic for longer and longer, increasing the hours of fitting staff and drafting in women for labouring jobs, there was little prospect of maintaining a cleaning gang at any shed. Photograph H.C. Casserley.

'Smoke Deflector Plates' is noted only on some Cards, to various Order Nos.; 6231 for instance got its plates in the period ending 7 September 1946, at a cost of £45.

Speed Indicators

'Speedometers' were a thorny subject. Instruments (mounted on a cumbersome hanging bracket) were certainly fitted to 6220-6224 and others, too, it seems. On 27 October 1937 the Mechanical and Electrical Engineering Committee had approved the fitting of 998 express locomotives with speed indicators. The outlook seemed good then: '*In view of additional restrictions imposed by the Chief Civil Engineer in relation to the maximum permissible speeds due to the introduction and increase of the*

accelerated express passenger services, consideration had been given to the desirability of fitting an instrument which would both indicate and make a continuous record of a speed of a locomotive and 20 express engines had been fitted with such a device under the authority of Traffic Committee Minute 5016 and Mechanical and Electrical Engineering Committee Minute 1098

Happier days, and a red 6226 DUCHESS OF NORFOLK hurries along with the ex-LNW Royal train. The stirring Duchess names gave rise to another popular term for the class and 'the Duchesses' they remain for many of us.

The red and the blue at Polmadie, 29 August 1938. 6227 DUCHESS OF DEVONSHIRE at the front, blue 6223 PRINCESS ALICE behind. 6223 had been in works twice since being built the year before, though it probably would not have been repainted. 6227 is more or less new but it still demonstrates something of the fundamental differences in the livery. Red 'wore' better than blue. Blue, as ever, weathered less well than red and suffered premature fading and streaking. It did not 'age' well, as BR learned all over again with the diesels many years later. Photograph T.G. Hepburn, Rail Archive Stephenson.

but it was not proposed to recommend the fitting of speed recorders generally owing to possible margins of error and the difficulty and cost of checking such records. It was however recommended that an electrical type of speed indicator be fitted to 998 locomotives working express passenger trains at an approximate estimated outlay of £23,000'.

Under wartime conditions it proved impossible to maintain and service the instruments. The fitting of 'electrical speed indicators' (as they were termed) on all the 998 engines projected in 1937 had been discontinued owing to shortage of materials and staff and the indicators (fitted to approximately 400 locos) had been taken off and the material placed in store. The

Mechanical and Electrical Engineering Committee heard on 29 January 1947 that *'since the cessation of hostilities the question of refitting the speed recorders and indicators had been reconsidered and it was recommended that the speed recorders should not be replaced and the speed indicators should be fitted to 366 locos of the following classes: class 7 4-6-2, class 6 4-6-0 ('Royal*

Talking of the unclad Coronations, Cecil J. Allen wrote in British Pacific Locomotives that 'No express passenger locomotives in Great Britain had a more stately and impressive appearance than these massive machines' And few would argue with that, marvelling at 46231 DUCHESS OF ATHOLL, in blue at Polmadie on 22 August 1953. Photograph J. Robertson, B.P. Hoper Collection.

6234 DUCHESS OF ABERCORN on the Polmadie turntable about 1947. Though hardly apparent through the grime, the engine is in the curious 'experimental' grey livery, applied to this particular locomotive only, in March 1946. Apparently the grey had maroon and straw lining. The five non-streamlined engines, 6230-6234, kept the draping front of the footplate ahead of the cylinders and so the nature of the smoke deflectors here was also different. Photograph W. Hermiston, B.P. Hoper Collection.

Scot'), class 6 4-6-0 (5X converted), 5X 4-6-0. During the time the speed indicators were fitted certain defects developed which were under consideration with Messrs. British Thomson Houston with a view to their elimination before refitting commenced and immediately these defects had been removed a report setting out the modified proposals, together with the cost of the work already carried out would be submitted'.

This report is unfortunately lost to us, but the prominent 'speedos', driven off the left hand trailing crank pin, were not generally fitted (46256 and 46257 apparently were equipped from new) until 1957, under Order No.R7461. A typical entry on the Record Cards in that year reads '28.12.57 Prov. of Speed Indicators £151.12.0'.

Cab Windows
The 'de-streamlined' engines required larger cab windows and these were fitted between 1948 and 1952. The work is hardly noted at all in the Record Cards, though one diligent scribe recorded the job on 6239's Card: 'Fitting of Larger Cab Windows' is noted for 23 June 1951, though no costs or Order No. are given. The work refers to the front window, and those on streamlined and newly 'de-streamlined' engines are noticeably narrower than on other engines.

46224 PRINCESS ALEXANDRA in blue, at Polmadie on 13 June 1948. The chalked inscription on the smokebox door reads *DOOR TIGHT 12/6/48.* A number of interpretations might be possible, but probably it was the Fireman, who had fully tightened the door, telling the preparing Fireman not to bother. Photograph James Stevenson.

That distinctive tender, on 6238 CITY OF CARLISLE. It is a former streamlined tender, marked by the centre ladder for access and the lack of a conventional step bracket at the rear running plate, and also the two tender filler caps, just visible with their handles. They had to be positioned like this on the streamlined tenders of course, for the hose was only got in (with some awkwardness and long years of swearing) through those sliding hatches which can be seen at the rear of the streamlined tenders. Tenders built 'conventionally' had the usual central filler and side steps by the rear axle box. The vestigial rearward extension of the sides was also a feature of the former streamlined tenders—indicated by the four angle brackets. On such tenders the downward curve at the front was higher up than on their 'conventional' brethren. The box with its two pipes leading up is of course, the coal pusher and its exhaust, while the little box with two pipes high up on the right-hand side was its siphon lubricator, both for the valves and the main ram piston.

locos the side sheets were extended back to close off the gap (so disruptive to airflow) between the rear of the tender and the front of the first coach. Sliding doors in the top of this faring allowed access for the water column hoses. The tenders were welded rather than riveted, which reduced weight by about a ton. Welding was continuous where water tightness was necessary but elsewhere intermittent welding was adopted. By proceeding like this distortion was minimised, though according to *The Railway Gazette* (*The Metallurgy of a High-Speed Locomotive*, 18 and 25 February 1938): '...*there was an inherent distortion in the side plates, where the gussets were welded on, causing small ridges to form on the outside of the plate. These ridges were ground off by portable hand-operated*

Tenders

The LMS built a ten ton tender, No.9359, with coal pusher in 1936, attaching it to Princess Royal 4-6-2 No.6206. It remained the only one so fitted among the Princess Royal Pacifics and it could only be operated

with 6206 (due to the different steam brake pipe between engine and tender). However, the principle was borne in mind and ten ton tenders with steam operated coal pushers were provided for the Coronations from the first. On the streamlined

The locomotives ran relatively briefly without those wonderful smoke deflectors—so vast, and yet there was still room to put the nameplate somewhere else! 6251 CITY OF NOTTINGHAM makes a fascinating contrast with local LMS built '60' Class No.14630, at Polmadie on 27 October 1945. Photograph H.C. Casserley.

From 1939 the streamliners looked increasingly scruffy and their looks suffered disproportionately from application of the black livery. Some of course, went into black straight from the Erecting Shop. Their appearance by the end of the War was a long way indeed from the shimmering electric blue and red-gold visions of the 1930s. The effect was further blighted by the long trailing trains of heterogeneous stock they were dragging around the country by this time. 46243 CITY OF LANCASTER (passing Berkhamsted on 7 May 1948) was the only streamliner to run under BR and in this picture was only weeks away from losing its casing. Photograph H.C. Casserley.

grinding tools when the tank was completed'. Welding (it was dearer) went out of fashion and the last five, the post-War engines, had distinctive riveted tenders.

The streamlined tenders had a cowl at the front, matching the outline of the cab roof, though at first the 1937 batch, 6220-6224, did not have this. Tenders for the non-streamlined engines (naturally enough) did not have the cowl though the non-streamlined 6249-6252 went into traffic with 'partially streamlined' tenders, which had already been built in anticipation of

more streamlined locomotives. Streamlining duly went and the tenders were similarly 'de-frocked'. The rear sheets began to disappear in the War years for reasons of access but with 'de-streamlining' more or less all trace went, so that all tenders appeared much the same. The only really noticeable difference lay in the shape at the front, where it met the cab. On most the tender front was cut away high up, matching the inward curve of the tender tops. This was the case with all the streamlined engines and the later conventional ones but the first conventional batch,

6230-6234, had a lower 'sweep', and so did the last two, 6256 and 46257. Former streamlined tenders were recognisable by the vestigial sheeting at the rear, extending back by an inch or two, and the access ladder.

Liveries
In nothing so much as livery did the Coronations exhibit change and differences, in abandon; Rowledge makes the eyebrow-raising comment that, of the *eleven* liveries used among this class of 38 locomotives, the constantly changing swirl of colour stood still sufficiently long for

The New Look. 46257 CITY OF SALFORD at Polmadie 24 May 1952, its shortened cab now bearing 8P. Apart from the technical innovations designed to achieve longer periods in revenue earning traffic, the roller bearings and rocking grate, self-cleaning smokebox and self-emptying ashpans, the superheating was brought to levels not so far seen in Britain, nearly a 1,000sq.ft. Photograph James Stevenson.

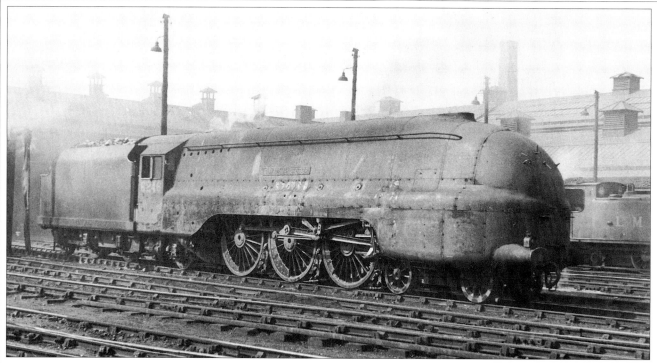

Faded glory hardly begins to describe poor, tired and faded 6246 CITY OF MANCHESTER, at Polmadie on 8 June 1946. Its case was removed in the autumn of that year. A relief, you might say. Photograph James Stevenson.

LIVERY CHANGES

No	First Liv.	War. black	Exp grey	LMS black	BR black	BR blue	BR green	BR red
6220	Blue	3/44	-	10/46	-	1/50	8/52	-
6221	Blue	8/44	-	7/46	-	2/50*	1/52	-
6222	Blue	10/44	-	5/46	-	9/50*	12/52	-
6223	Blue	2/44	-	8/46	-	3/50	9/52	-
6224	Blue	10/44	-	7/46	-	5/48#	4/52	-
6225	Red	4/44	-	3/47	-	2/50	2/53	8/58
6226	Red	?/44	-	6/47	11/48	5/49	4/51*	11/58
6227	Red	1/44	-	3/47	-	5/48#	5/53	-
6228	Red	4/44	-	11/47	-	8/50	8/55	6/58
6229	Red	8/43*	-	12/47	-	1/50*	3/52	9/58
6230	Red	-	-	9/46	-	5/48#	3/52	-
6231	Red	8/45*	-	9/46	-	5/48#	11/53	-
6232	Red	2/45	-	9/47	-	-	11/51*	-
6233	Red	-	-	9/46	-	-	12/52*	-
6234	Red	-	3/46	-	-	5/48#	1/52	-
6235	Red	3/43	-	4/46	-	10/50*	4/53	-
6236	Red	4/44	-	12/47	-	-	8/55	7/58
6237	Red	8/43*	-	2/47	-	8/49*	8/52*	-
6238	Red	?/43	-	8/46	3/49	-	10/53	6/58
6239	Red	3/44*	-	9/47	-	6/50*	7/54*	-
6240	Red	11/45	-	7/47	-	1/50	9/54*	7/58
6241	Red	5/43*	-	2/47	-	5/48#	4/53*	-
6242	Red	5/44	-	5/47	-	8/49	11/53	-
6243	Red	1/44	-	-	-	6/49	1/54*	10/58
6244	Red	1/44	-	8/47	-	9/48#	5/53	10/58
6245	Black	New	-	11/47	-	-	4/53	12/57
6246	Black	New	-	11/46	11/48	-	5/53*	10/58
6247	Black	New	-	2/47	-	-	1/54*	5/58
6248	Black	New	-	1/47	3/49	-	8/53*	6/58
6249	Black	New	-	11/46	-	8/50*	1/53*	-
6250	Black	New	-	7/47	-	3/50*	9/52*	-
6251	Black	New	-	6/47	4/49	-	10/51*	11/58
6252	Black	New	-	11/46*	3/49	?/50	1/54*	-
6253	Black	-	-	New	-	-	10/53*	-
6254	Black	-	-	New	-	8/50*	1/53*	9/58
6255	Black	-	-	New	-	6/50	4/53	-
6256	Black	-	-	New	11/48	3/51*	5/54*	5/58
6257	Black	-	-	-	New	-	11/52*	-

Table adapted from Rowledge (The LMS Pacifics, D&C 1987), with kind permission.

*approximate—probably into service some weeks later

#'experimental' blue when first painted

46236, 46256 and 46257 ran with tenders lettered BRITISH RAILWAYS

only one—BR lined green, from August 1955 to December 1957—to be applied to the whole class at the same time! Summarised, liveries were blue, then red, for the streamlined and non-streamlined engines until 1943, when wartime black was brought in. Most got this plain black in 1944, one or two not until early 1945. 6245-6252, new from 1943 onwards, were plain 'wartime' black from new.

Apart from an experimental grey on 6234 in 1946 the next general livery was LMS lined black, then the BR black with LNWR lining. All were in one form of black, wartime, LMS or BR, when BR introduced the famous blue (in different shades) which most had got by 1950-51. All got the succeeding BR green in the early 1950s and there then came the celebrated reversion to red, when sixteen Coronations received LMS-style crimson lake—BR's 'maroon'. (There were two different lining styles with the maroon livery, the older LMS-type later being exclusive.) The table left, taken from Rowledge's *The LMS Pacifics* (David & Charles 1987) and reproduced with kind permission,

You'll Remember those Black and White Days...

OVER THERE

In the highly inauspicious year of 1939, a Coronation Pacific and a train of LMS stock built for the Coronation Scot journeyed across the Atlantic to be the British representative at the New York World's Fair. 6220 CORONATION looked bonny indeed with its light and bell, except of course, that the engine was in fact 6229 DUCHESS OF HAMILTON. CORONATION merely donated its plates and numbers, assuming the identity of 6229 for the duration, back in the home country. It wasn't that the engine was indisposed, it was just that the PR people (rightly) preferred a red and gold engine—and that is how 'CORONATION' came to run in red, and 'DUCHESS OF HAMILTON' in blue! The whole ensemble departed from Southampton, courtesy of the Southern Railway, to be delivered onto the Baltimore & Ohio. Obviously a suitably dramatic picture should be available at the earliest possible opportunity, to publicise its extensive tour from 21 March to 14 April, taking in Baltimore, Washington, Pittsburgh, Chicago and many other cities (prior to landing up at New York for the Fair). This photograph, taken from the air with a cunningly inserted four engined aircraft (pretty much out of scale) would fit the bill. That allotment shed, and the lack of the bell alerts us to the fact that the scene could hardly be *less* transAtlantic; it turns out to be near Watford...

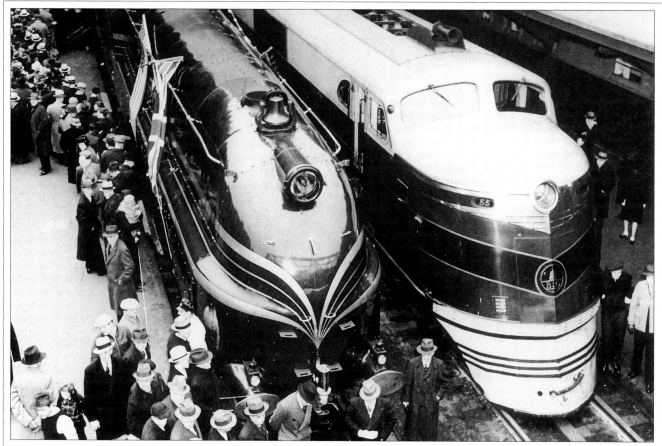

Truly Over There. A familiar picture, with '6220' posed with a Baltimore & Ohio diesel at Baltimore on 18 March 1939. Riddles was in charge of the tour, and apparently the coal provided came as something of a shock, for it was the sort of slack customarily supplied to US locomotives, with their vast maws and mechanical stokers. With the Driver (Freddie Bishop of Camden) going down with pneumonia, Riddles had taken a good share of the firing and was more than once engaged in frantic repair work. Riddles gave an address to the Junior Institution of Engineers in which he described burning eleven or twelve tons of coal ('or dirt!') in *one* day. Improvisation was the order of the day, turning up parts to fit and spending nights working on a fallen brick arch. Filthy and exhausted, it was then a case of negotiating entry into the hotel. Extricating a brick arch means manoeuvring something weighing (in its myriad parts) near enough a ton inside a fearsomely hot firebox. Riddles afterwards certainly deserved his *'bath, rump steak, bottle of champagne and bed'*.

charts the myriad changes. An oddity was 46239 CITY OF CHESTER. It must have presented a peculiar sight in July 1950 when, 'owing to the incidence of Works Holidays' it was sent into traffic for four days 'unpainted'.

The Last Two: Rocking Grates, Roller Bearings and 100,000 Miles a Year

The major departure in appearance, after the streamlining/de-streamlining process, came with the last two Coronations of 1947-48, built at least in part as a means of comparison with Ivatt's new diesels, 10000 and 10001 and described earlier.

It was hoped to push mileages through to 100,000 per year with the last two Coronations, 6256 and 46257, extending the shopping period at the same time from about eight months to twelve months. The rocking grate, self cleaning smokebox and hopper ashpans, now becoming the standard across the LMS/LMR/BR, would increase availability and manganese steel linings and grease roller bearings on all axles, engine and tender would, it was hoped, be the means of

extending the annual mileage. (They weren't.)

The trailing truck on the last two was very different, and the main reason for the visual differences. The whole rear end was redesigned, with the old framing replaced by a sort of bar frame extension; the new Delta truck looked very different and meant that the cab sides could be reduced, losing the attractive curved bottom to the cab.

The three Coronations built in 1946, 6253-6255, had got rocking grates, following the revelations of American practice and on 29 January 1947 the Mechanical and Electrical Engineering Committee recommended fitting self-cleaning smokeboxes as well as *'proper ashpans and rocking grates on 33 class 7 4-6-2 passenger locomotives of the Coronation class'*. At that time there were actually thirty-six Coronations in service but 6253-6255 had already got the rocking grates and self-cleaning smokeboxes; 6256 and 6257, with the long-envisaged 'experimental features' were yet to be built.

The report continues: *'The fitting of rocking grates - a feature adopted as standard on all new*

engines - will assist in keeping the fire clean when the engines are working long distance expresses. Ashpans of the hopper type were already fitted to 20 of the engines and the remaining 13 would be similarly fitted as a necessary adjunct to the rocking grate. Controls inside the cab would also be provided to facilitate the emptying of the ashpans under varying operating conditions. The self cleaning smokebox keeps the lower row of tubes free from obstruction and assists disposal of the engines by avoiding the necessity to clean out the smokebox each day. Estimate £9,085. Approved'.

Double Chimney

It is not always present, but many of the Record Cards have a reference, under Order No.6865, *'Double Blastpipe and Chimney'* at about £70. As an experiment, a double blastpipe and chimney had been fitted to 6234 DUCHESS OF ABERCORN; witness the engine's storming progress with twenty coaches from Crewe to Carlisle and back, described under the section chronicling the 1938 building of 6225-6234. The engine had been tested a fortnight before on the same working, with its original single chimney, and had failed to keep steam and time. So the triumph with the double arrangement a couple of weeks later was all the more telling. No.6235, and all the engines after it, were given the new double chimney, and the earlier engines were modified as soon afterwards as maybe. Rowledge (*The LMS Pacifics*, David & Charles, 1987) has an amusing story of 6245 having a Kylchap exhaust when new in 1943, the story being that it had come from the LNER at Doncaster, though it had also been in the possession of the Southern at Eastleigh... It was removed when someone noticed that CITY OF LONDON didn't sound like the rest... Allen (*British Pacific Locomotives*) makes the point that the double chimney as fitted to the class as a whole was *not* a Kylchap arrangement. The Kylchap on the LNER was a series of petticoats, one below the other between the base of the chimney and the blast orifices. The arrangement on the Coronations was simpler, the blastpipe branching into two with the two chimneys, in line, sited above.

Bits and Pieces

A typical Record Card, under the heading 'Improvements, Etc.' might read (without quoting Order Nos.) something like: (*see table right*).

After this, improvement work is usually noted simply with the Crewe Order No., 'E4176, R7481' and so on. The Cards were maintained by

different people at different times and there is no strict continuity to the entries. It *is* possible, by cross referencing, to discover what some of these Order Nos. are. 46225 for instance got its speed indicator under Order R7461 on 5.10.57 at the incredible cost of £322.19.3. (Some of the costings look a mite problematical; they are given as two sums, under Capital and Revenue accounts and sometimes the figures are added together to give the total, other times they subtracted...) But to return to the detective work: 46224 for instance has no 'speedo' listed but has the same (anonymous) number R7461, the same date and more or less the same cost, so it is quite possible to date its speedo fitting, too.

Other references are more obscure, however, and often earlier improvements such as double chimneys and smoke deflectors are difficult to trace. 46228, for instance, has a listing '17.9.40 X6865 Double Blast Pipe & Chimney £62.3.9'. 46229 has the same Order No. and

description but the date is 15.5.43 and the cost £126.0.0. On other Cards there is just the Order No. or no reference at all. Smoke deflectors are hard to find; there is no reference to them at all in most cards and the job did not have an Order No. to enable a cross reference. 6234 is noted getting its deflectors in the period ending 10.8.46, at £45, but the heading is that famous one, 'Misc.'.

Other, apparently minor jobs, are consistently recorded, and in some detail, such as 'removal of sand guns' and 'tell-tale device to give warning of excessive heating of inside big-ends'. The first was a steam jet operated by the crew, intended to 'free-up' the tubes from the firebox end. It directed a blast of sand through the tubes to clean them but the debris went up through the chimney, and onto Mrs Jones' washing! It proved ineffective and was taken out from the Coronations about 1952. The 'stink bomb' was just that, and gave off an unmistakable odour when the big

'2.9.44 New design valves, casing and filter for oil relief valves	£3.12.6
28.3.45 Flexible pipe to sand hopper	£1.14.0
13.7.46 Misc.	£103.0.0
29.11.47 Longer dis. Monel Stays	£12.0.0.
27.12.47 Fitting of small Radius Rocking Washers and new bottom frame bars	£47.7.7
15.5.48 Prov. of additional washout plugs	£1.15.0
29.11.52 Removal of sand guns and equipment	£1.7.0'

On tour at Hartford, Connecticut. More than two million people viewed the train but it was not possible to get it away before War broke out. The locomotive eventually made its way back, to Cardiff, in February 1942, though the coaches had to await the peace. If DUCHESS OF HAMILTON had been lost at sea (and there was every likelihood) would the real Duchess, running back home as CORONATION, have remained thus? When Ivatt built his two Pacifics, would one have taken up the missing number? Would our Ian Allan *Combined Volumes* have forever had the number 46220 missing? Or would it have been 46229? Exquisite questions! Photograph G.W. Goslin Collection.

The British Railways Locomotive Interchange Trials of 1948 are well-chronicled, and so is the fact that the Stanier Pacific probably showed less well than it could. Certainly this was the case with 46236 CITY OF BRADFORD on the Southern. Driver Byford, it is said, was concerned with coal consumption rather than dramatic flourishes. Allen in his book *The Locomotive Exchanges 1870-1948* (Ian Allan, 1949) tells of all the Pacifics on the Southern testing ground, A4, Merchant Navy and 46236, being trounced by Royal Scot 46154 THE HUSSAR, so it was an LM victory of sorts! 46236 (seen here at Waterloo) was notable for the attachment of a WD tender, for greater water capacity on the Southern, which lacked troughs. The LMS had never owned such tenders but in despite of this, and the fact that CITY OF BRADFORD was already numbered in its BR sequence (something which seems to have been insisted upon) someone saw a loophole and hurriedly had the tender lettered LMS... The Record Card incidentally, shows it to have been off a Western Region WD, numbered A79294. Photograph C.C.B. Herbert.

end to which it was attached grew too hot. These were fitted about 1951.

'Additional clothing on inside cylinders' was another general entry; it was also one of the few jobs which can be matched to the LMS Engineering Minutes. There are few original references to, say, double chimneys or smoke deflectors, though certainly there would have been reports, assessments, approvals and all the rest. However, so far as the cylinders are concerned there is for once a Mechanical and Electrical Engineering Committee reference: *'22 March 1945 recommend 29 4-6-2 locomotives be fitted with additional cylinder clothing to the inside cylinders at an estimated cost of £810 to prevent the bad effect of cold air which was at present drawn up over the steam chest of the inside cylinder and which it was thought was partly responsible for certain amount of cracking in the cylinders'.*

AWS/ATC
Despite CITY OF LEICESTER's derailment at Polesworth in 1951 (see under the locomotive's separate entry), in which the Inspecting Officer once again recommended Automatic Train Control (or AWS-Automatic Warning System) it was nearly a decade before the big LM express engines got it. It was a prominent feature, for it had to be protected from the front screw coupling by a substantial shield; there were also air reservoirs and battery box to be accommodated on the footplating. Some engines, no doubt, would have carried this long-overdue improvement for only three years or so.

A Note on Record Cards
Several points were made above regarding the various inconsistencies which litter the Record Cards. This is hardly to be marvelled at, for the cards were kept over a quarter of a century, by different people in different places; there was a war on for much of the period and after 1948 the line which had operated the Coronations from their construction was divided into two separate organisations, very much independent of each other. The Coronations appeared before the Second World War and the last of them came in the first year of BR. Much policy and practice changed over that time, a new form of card was devised, headings changed, emphasis varied. So a lot changed (though a lot didn't!) and many of the inconsistencies in the record seem to owe as much to accident as much as anything else. Mileages and building costs seem to vary in the rigour with which they are recorded and as we have seen, some major items, such as smoke deflectors and double chimneys are altogether absent from some cards.

The Record Cards, anomalously, give *two* dates for removal of streamlining; one is taken from the day off Crewe for the particular works visit in which the casing was removed and it is reported again (though not always...) under *'Improvements etc.'*. This relates to 'period ending' and is by definition later. Again by definition, the first date (the one used in this book) is more accurate.

Boilers are fairly well detailed, but some cards begin the record (presumably as practice changed over the years) with the first boiler carried by the locomotive, other cards begin with the first *change* of boiler—comparison with the building date will reveal this. In the first years the records are more interesting, for when a new boiler is fitted the 'donor' locomotive (that is, the locomotive which previously bore the overhauled boiler) is also recorded. Other items are flatly incomprehensible. What does *'deleted from selected list 20.1.58'* mean, for instance, on Scottish ones only?

The record is often abandoned before the end—1955 in the case of 46220, when it clearly would have had several more boilers after that—and continues odd procedural points such as '(EO)' after the reference. This is thought to mean 'Engine Order' though quite what it signifies is unknown. Could it be 'Engine Only'? Answers on a postcard please...

Total mileage is recorded; but not right to the bitter end. In any event it was an estimation, a minor miracle of paperwork and not mechanically recorded.

Prices quoted differ over the years, for it took a long time to build the Coronations. There are some amusing differences, however. The early engines were priced at £10,095, which seems specific enough, but 6222, apparently, cost 8/11d more!

Allocations are not perfectly recorded, but the Record Card listings have been left as they are, rather than try and amend them by reference to other published material. The Camden Pacifics, or most of them, went to Willesden as Camden was reorganised for diesels and these transfers, for instance, do not always show in the record. (See 46239's picture, brooding and dark-

lit, with its 1A plate.) It plainly went to Willesden, yet there is no mention in the Card; the maintenance of records was already becoming a lost art. Some of the late transfers to Kingmoor are similarly lost.

A Note on Codes
Precisely what degree of work constituted a particular grade of repair varied over the years, especially between LMS and BR practice, and between pre-Group/early LMS and later LMS practice. LMS codes, in the time of the Coronations, were as follows:
HG Heavy General; **NC** Non Classified. **LS** and **HS** stood for Light Service and Heavy Service respectively. This 'Service' classification was replaced, broadly speaking, by the 'Intermediate' category. **LO** seems to stand for Light Overhaul, **TRO** for some forms of out of the ordinary shed repair.
By BR days, **HI** and **LI** meant Heavy Intermediate and Light Intermediate, while **HG** still meant Heavy General. **NC** stood for Non Classified.

****

Whatever their deficiencies, the Record Cards are a splendid record of what *actually happened* to these locomotives, and that is why they still exert such a fascination today. They form a goodly part of this account and very little of the vast information they contain has, to my knowledge, appeared in print before. The rest of the account is to an extent a

distillation of material that has long been published but it is married to original work at the Public Record Office Kew and at the National Railway Museum, so that a few new shafts of light at least, however dim, have fallen on the 'Big 'Uns', as only a true Crewe man is allowed to describe them. I've borrowed the phrase (from Allan Baker's *Crewe Sheds*, my first real insight into these locomotives) for, despite all the varied terms, from 'Big Lizzies' to 'Semis', to 'Coronations' to 'Duchesses' (*Doochesses* as the Edge Hill men called them) none has seemed more apt since my first, child's eye sight of one, CITY OF STOKE-ON-TRENT, from the footbridge at Camden shed in the 1950s. Nothing, up till then, had seemed *so big*.

It is this quality of majesty that I particularly hope to have conveyed in this account. It is not an engineering or operating treatise, though the views and comments of LMR men from both these specialisms are incorporated in it. Special thanks to: John Jennison of *Brassmasters* fame (exquisite etched brass kits of LMS prototypes—PO Box 1137, Sutton Coldfield, West Midlands, B76 1RG), Barry Hoper and Janet too, Alec Swain, Allan Baker (whose long-maturing account of the maintenance and operation of the Coronations is eagerly awaited), Peter Rowledge, Geoff Goslin, Stephen Summerson, Hamish Stevenson, Richard Hardy, Irving Nichol, Ashley Butlin, Ed Bartholomew and Phil Atkins.

CITY OF BRADFORD on an Up Plymouth train at West Ealing in April-May 1948. In the 1948 Interchange the big Pacific did well on some days on the Western Region and not so well on others. It was responsible for 'a most uninspiring run' on 19 May, but elsewhere showed moments of brilliance. It was but an interlude, and it was the experience and practice of the London Midland locomotive engineers that would chiefly guide British Railways in the matter of development and evolution from now on. Photograph National Railway Museum.

Roaring progress of the down Royal Scot at Motherwell with, appropriately, 46220 CORONATION. The date is 6 June 1953 and the engine is carrying the special adornment made up for the Coronation year. Photograph J. Robertson, B.P. Hoper Collection.

Repairs LMS	
1/11/37-18/11/37**LO**	10/9/42-3/10/42**LS**
4/4/38-14/4/38**LO**	16/4/43-14/5/43**HG**
22/9/38-19/10/38**LS**	11/2/44-11/3/44**HS**
27/3/39-6/4/39**LO**	20/4/44-19/5/44**LO**
29/11/39-5/1/40**HG**	30/4/45-2/6/45**LS**
22/2/40-19/3/40**LO**	4/10/45-9/11/45**LO**
3/8/40-24/8/40**LO**	26/9/46-6/11/46**HG**
5/11/40-10/12/40**LO**	3/6/48-3/7/48**LS**
5/3/41-22/3/41**LO**	20/7/48-3/7/48**TRO**
21/7/41-16/8/41**HS**	10/1/49-12/2/49**HC**
7/1/42-5/2/42**LO**	12/12/49-26/1/50**HG**
	18/7/50-18/8/50**LC**

46220 CORONATION

Built Crewe 1/6/37, cost £10,095 (engine), £1,546 (tender)
Renumbered 6229 ('verbal message CME') 20/12/38
Renumbered 6220 ('during repairs at Crewe') April 1943
Built streamlined, casing removed 6/11/46
Renumbered 6220 to 46220 week ending 3/7/48

LMS 'Summary' (this became 'Annual Statistics' from 1951)

Year	Mileage	wks	shed	n/req	total
1937	36,210	9	31	21	61
1938	66,809	34	52	22	108
1939	67,907	37	60	24	133#
1940	54,901	78	37	22	137
1941	54,705	42	91	11	144
1942	71,104	47	36	10	93
1943	74,633	25	52	3	80
1944	40,435	52	93	2	147
1945	54,957	61	81	-	142
1946	48,435	36	117	1	154
1947	59,505	-	65	-	65
1948	46,006	27	80	2	109
1949	55,214	48	65	2	117
1950	66,906	47	48	-	95
1951	62,022	26	71	-	97
1952	49,359	91	38	-	129
1953	56,086	51	52	2	105
1954	55,535	37	44	-	81
1955	40,828	78	67	1	146
1956	61,050	-	62	1	63
1957	58,412	33	42	2	77

#includes 12 days 'stored unserviceable'
record ends
wks=heavy and light repairs at main works
shed=shed repairs and examinations
n/req= not required

Total Recorded Mileage 1,178,019
Withdrawn week ending 20/4/63
Cut up Crewe Works 5/63

Repairs BR
[Dates in first column are from out of traffic to return to traffic; the two 'mileage' figures represent, firstly the miles accumulated since the previous General or Intermediate and secondly (the lower figure) the miles run up from January 1st of the year of shopping. All are recorded as taking place at Crewe unless otherwise noted. StR=St Rollox]

Dates	Weekdays Waiting	Weekdays On Works	Mileage	'Jan 1' Mileage
19/4/51-19/5/51**LI**	3	23	85,096	18,190
15/5/52-29/8/52**G**	10	81	67,479	23,647
23/4/53-21/5/53**LC***	6	19	46,771	21,059
12/10/53-11/11/53**LI**	6	20	73,331	47,711
1/9/54-1/9/54**NC**	-	1(StR)	52,905	44,530
22/9/54-4/11/54**LC***	12	25	56,504	48,129
24/5/55-30/7/55**G**	9	49	79,668	15,778
2/8/55-25/8/55**NC***	-	20	nil	15,778
12/2/57-22/3/57**LI**	6	27	93,572	7,472
25/11/57-28/11/57**NC**	-	3	-	-
19/5/58-26/6/58**HI**	1	34	72,235	21,295

record ends
*='(EO)' - 'Engine Only'

Sheds
Camden	1/6/37
Rugby	16/9/39
Camden	21/10/39
Polmadie	21/12/39
Polmadie	15/5/43
Crewe North	13/7/56

stored 19/9/39 to 2/10/39

Tenders
No	Fitted
9703	1/6/37
9803	23/6/44
9703	6/8/44
9804	9/1/46
9705	3/8/49

Boilers
Fitted	No.	From
5/1/40	10637	new
1/5/43	9939	6223
6/11/46	10292	6243
26/1/50	10640	6242
29/8/52	10302	-
30/7/55	10295	-

No record after this date

6220 CORONATION out on the road. Anxious to wrest every publicity advantage from the new streamliners, the LMS arranged for a film to be made. For two hours in the early morning of Sunday 13 June 1937 all four lines between Llandudno Junction and Colwyn Bay were closed so that 6220 with the Coronation Scot could be filmed running abreast of the 1911 Coronation train hauled by George V No.25348, and the Liverpool & Manchester Railway replica train hauled by LION. It must have been a truly astonishing sight, with the fourth line occupied by Class 2P No.695 with a brake van and something called a scenery truck, 'overtaking or running parallel with the trains as required'.
Photograph M.W.Earley.

CORONATION at Polmadie on 6 July 1957. A Camden engine during its streamlined 1930s days, as 6229 DUCHESS OF HAMILTON it went to Polmadie on the outbreak of war, staying there until the middle 1950s, by which time of course it had been renumbered and named back to CORONATION. The 'Scottish' blue ground to the nameplate was very quickly changed to black on its return to Crewe! Photograph J. Robertson, B.P. Hoper Collection.

46220 at Polmadie, March 1959. A Crewe North engine by now, along with the rest of the 'big 'uns' there, it was engaged in night diagrams north to Glasgow and Perth on sleepers, mails and newspaper trans. This was one reason why they could sometimes seem so scarce at Euston itself—maddeningly so at times. Photograph J. Robertson, B.P. Hoper Collection.

The air thickens over Polmadie shed on a wet lighting up afternoon in March 1959. The water hose is 'in' one of the twin fillers dating from the streamliner days. Photograph J. Robertson, B.P. Hoper Collection.

Ranging the length of the West Coast and still a Crewe North 'big 'un', 46220 at Willesden, March 1959. Photograph Alec Swain, B. P. Hoper Collection.

46221 as 'Semi', 22 September 1951, at Glasgow St Enoch. The term was an enthusiast one and seems to have established a far greater currency in the years since the engines' demise than it ever enjoyed during their working lives. In most enthusiast circles, the appearance of the shaved-off smokeboxes was a bit of a shock, and the term 'Semi' was the last to come to mind. After all, the new engines were definitely not streamlined in any way, nor (it was obvious) were they intended to be. It would be fascinating to know where and when the term was first coined; presumably there is a precise moment when it appeared in print for the first time? Photograph J. Robertson, B.P. Hoper Collection.

46221 QUEEN ELIZABETH

Built Crewe 14/6/37 cost £10,095 (engine), £1,546 (tender)
Built streamlined, casing removed 28/6/46
Renumbered 6221 to 46221 week ending 23/10/48

Repairs LMS

17/2/38-1/3/38**LO**	15/6/44-29/7/44**LS**
27/6/38-1/7/38**TO**	17/4/45-12/5/45**LS**
24/10/38-15/11/38**LS**	22/5/46-28/6/46**HG**
18/4/39-27/4/39**LO**	24/1/47-1/2/47**LO**
7/8/39-29/8/39**LS**	21/3/47-5/5/47**LO**
24/9/40-6/11/40**HG**	1/12/47-6/12/47**NC**
17/12/40-14/1/41**LO**	16/9/48-22/10/48**HS**
7/7/41-9/8/41**LO**	8/1/49-1/2/49**LC**
11/2/42-11/3/42**LS**	13/5/49-17/6/49**LC**
26/9/42-31/10/42**HS**	28/9/49-29/10/49**LC**
9/6/43-17/7/43**HG**	13/2/50-30/3/50**HG**

Repairs BR

[Dates in first column are from out of traffic to return to traffic; the two 'mileage' figures represent, firstly the miles accumulated since the previous General or Intermediate and secondly (the generally lower figure) the miles run up from January 1st of the year of shopping. All are recorded as taking place at Crewe unless otherwise noted. StR=St Rollox]

Dates	Weekdays Waiting	Weekdays On Works	Mileage	'Jan 1' Mileage
26/2/51-5/4/51**LI**	5	28	81,258	15,139
12/2/52-7/4/52**HI**	3	44	69,343	8,843
2/7/52-20/8/52**LC***	15	27	17,933	26,776
30/10/52-16/12/52**HG**	5	35	29,521	38,364
23/2/54-3/4/54**HI**	7	27	69,174	5,691
24/12/54-24/12/54**NC***	-	(StR)	-	57,706
24/2/55-24/2/55**NC**	-	(StR)	-	46,005
24/9/55-5/11/55**HG**	5	31	90,412	43,811
23/7/56-1/9/56**LC***	12	23	42,573	36,016
28/9/57-9/11/57**LI**	4	32	102,387	39,459
17/11/58-1/1/59**HI**	4	33	69,566	63,922
10/9/59-30/10/59**LC**	16	27	59,885	59,885
1/5/60-7/6/60**HI**	3	28	105,310	33,288
19/6/61-7/9/61**HG**	30	39	66,618	22,263

record ends
*='(EO)' - 'Engine Only'

Sheds

Camden	19/6/37
Crewe North	16/9/39
Camden	21/10/39
Polmadie(loan)	25/11/39
Polmadie	30/12/39
Crewe North	5/7/58
Camden	20/6/59
Crewe North	1/10/60
Carlisle Upperby	7/4/62

Stored 10/9/39-2/10/39, and 29/10/62 to we 2/2/63

Tenders

No	Fitted
9704	14/6/37
9816	17/11/61
9359	18/10/62

LMS 'Summary' *(this became 'Annual Statistics' from 1951)*

Year	Mileage	Weekdays out of service			
		wks	shed	n/req	total
1937	30,945	-	37	20	57
1938	67,705	36	39	15	90
1939	66,484	29	46	29	128#
1940	74,123	49	43	31	123
1941	61,882	43	73	12	128
1942	68,199	56	38	5	99
1943	68,945	34	61	2	97
1944	71,847	39	63	3	105
1945	53,202	22	110	2	134
1946	67,947	33	80	2	115
1947	52,165	47	68	2	117
1948	57,948	32	66	1	99
1949	49,494	80	51	2	133
1950	71,441	39	46	-	85
1951	75,639	33	69	-	102
1952	40,424	129	30	1	160
1953	61,423	-	80	-	80
1954	52,292	34	88	3	125
1955	50,368	36	54	12	102
1956	56,371	35	43	1	79
1957	45,103	35	80	2	117
1958	63,922	34	38	-	72
1959	72,022				

#includes 24 days 'stored serviceable'
record ends
wks=heavy and light repairs at main works
shed=shed repairs and examinations
n/req= not required

Total Recorded Mileage 1,387,893
Withdrawn week ending 18/5/63
Cut up Crewe Works 7/63

Boilers

Fitted	No.	From
6/11/40	10303	6232
17/7/43	10637	6220
28/6/46	10294	6234
30/3/50	10694	6241
16/12/52	10292	-
5/11/55	10694	-
7/9/61	10298	-

No record after this date

QUEEN ELIZABETH on the Polmadie turntable, 18 May 1951, bright and shiny amid the broil of fume that otherwise so often cloaked the great Caledonian shed. The engine is in the curious 'Semi' state, for its smokebox was not brought to normal condition for another year. Clearly, there is no speed indicator now fitted; these were to come (all together, in something of a rush) in 1957. Photograph J. Robertson, B.P. Hoper Collection.

Coronation Pacifics

Repairs LMS	10/4/46-24/5/46LS
15/6/38-28/6/38LO	14/1/47-28/2/47LO
5/12/38-22/12/38LS	5/5/47-31/7/47HS
2/12/39-24/1/40HG	11/8/47-14/8/47NC
25/1/41-20/2/41LS	7/10/47-11/10/47NC
21/5/42-20/6/42HS	17/8/48-21/9/48LS
11/6/43-28/7/43HG	22/7/49-15/9/49LI
6/7/44-5/8/44LS	16/9/49-22/9/49NC
11/6/45-28/7/45HG	20/2/50-17/3/50LC
1/3/46-16/3/46LO	29/8/50-28/10/50G

46222 QUEEN MARY

Built Crewe 22/6/37, cost £10,095 8s 11d (engine), £1,546 (tender)
Built streamlined, casing removed 10/7/46
Renumbered 6222 to 46222 week ending 25/9/48

LMS 'Summary' *(this became 'Annual Statistics' from 1951)*

Year	Mileage	wks	shed	n/req	total
1937	33,300	-	24	23	47
1938	69,163	28	37	28	93
1939	67,299	24	76	9	109
1940	83,546	21	51	28	100
1941	50,329	23	100	6	129
1942	61,516	27	62	5	94
1943	56,720	41	109	3	153
1944	70,665	27	96	6	129
1945	58,493	42	96	2	140
1946	55,946	53	112	3	168
1947	42,531	120	30	-	150
1948	61,078	31	52	-	83
1949	61,093	54	49	1	104
1950	55,828	74	38	1	113
1951	70,835	34	40	-	74
1952	67,193	50	59	-	109
1953	37,404	59	103	-	162
1954	64,424	-	50	-	50
1955	50,071	41	64	-	120
1956	60,629	30	53	-	86
1957	45,164	37	49	-	101
1958	45,726	20	93	-	113
1959	47,080		record ends		
1960	61,272				
1961	50,443				
1962	30,612				

wks=heavy and light repairs at main works
shed=shed repairs and examinations
n/req= not required

Total Recorded Mileage 1,458,368
Withdrawn week ending 26/10/63
Cut up Crewe Works 11/63

Repairs BR

[Dates in first column are from out of traffic to return to traffic; the two 'mileage' figures represent, firstly the miles accumulated since the previous General or Intermediate and secondly (the generally lower figure) the miles run up from January 1st of the year of shopping. All are recorded as taking place at Crewe unless otherwise noted. StR=St Rollox]

Dates	Weekdays Waiting	Weekdays On Works	Mileage	'Jan 1' Mileage
20/11/51-29/12/51LI6		28	87,165	70,835
30/4/52-27/6/52LC	6	44	26,008	26,008
4/6/53-12/8/53G	12	47	77,762	20,569
20/8/53-22/8/53NC	-	2	672	21,241
27/4/54-27/4/54NC*	-	1(StR)	38,706	21,871
7/9/54-8/9/54NC	-	1(StR)	61,835	45,000
26/2/55-16/4/55G	7	34	87,356	6,097
11/4/56-12/4/56NC	-	1(StR)	62,494	18,520
20/4/56-25/5/56HI	9	21	63,966	19,992
19/4/57-1/6/57HI	8	29	59,055	18,418
#4/6/57-10/6/57NC*	-	5	-	-
#4/6/57-19/6/57NC*	-	13	192	18,610
21/6/57-3/7/57NC*	-	10	248	18,666
2/12/57-4/12/57NC*	-	2	-	-
5/12/58-27/1/59G	14	29	72,472	45,726
14/7/59-13/11/59LC	23	33	39,464	39,464
5/9/60-19/10/60HI	6	32	93,401	46,321
26/4/61-17/6/61HC	10	35	34,697	19,746
26/3/62-28/7/62G	9	98	-	-

#†dates conflict; pres. clerical error
record ends
=‘(EO)' - 'Engine Only'

Sheds
Camden	22/6/37
Polmadie	21/11/39

Tenders
No	Fitted
9705	22/6/37
9804	3/8/49

Boilers
Fitted	No.	From
24/1/40	10638	new
28/7/43	10298	6227
28/7/45	10287	6233
9/8/47	10296	6242
28/10/50	12471	6254
12/8/53	10295	-
16/4/55	12472	-

No record after this date

46222 QUEEN MARY on Beattock, a 'Big Lizzie' in its natural haunts, the fell country of northern England and the Southern Uplands of Scotland. 26 June 1954. Photograph J. Robertson, B.P. Hoper Collection.

6223 PRINCESS ALICE at Carlisle. The 'Princess Coronations' were ground breaking things, carrying locomotive development to the limits of power and speed then possible within the given outline. Photograph B.P. Hoper Collection.

Repairs LMS

6/1/38-19/1/38**LO**	22/8/44-16/9/44**LS**
11/7/38-25/7/38**LS**	28/5/45-13/7/45**HG**
17/11/38-2/12/38**LO**	24/9/45-3/11/45**HO**
18/4/39-3/5/39**LS**	10/6/46-6/8/46**LS**
4/3/40-17/4/40**HG**	12/12/46-31/12/46**LO**
6/12/40-2/1/41**HS**	27/2/47-10/3/47**LO**
25/8/41-20/9/41**LO**	14/5/47-20/6/47**LS**
3/10/41-1/11/41**HG**	8/9/47-5/12/47**HO**
23/4/42-30/5/42**HO**	14/2/49-14/3/49**LI**
21/9/42-5/11/42**LO**	11/10/49-17/11/49**LC**
6/5/43-28/5/43**LS**	24/11/49-2/12/49**NC**
13/12/43-22/1/44**LS**	20/2/50-14/4/50**HG**

46223 PRINCESS ALICE

Built Crewe 28/6/37, cost £10,095 (engine), £1,546 (tender)
Built streamlined, casing removed 6/8/46
Renumbered 6223 to 46223 week ending 19/3/49

LMS 'Summary' (this became 'Annual Statistics' from 1951)

Year	Mileage	Weekdays out of service			
		wks	shed	n/req	total
1937	29,875	-	37	20	57
1938	66,968	39	43	27	109
1939	69,267	14	81	32	127
1940	61,786	58	37	18	113
1941	53,227	53	68	6	127
1942	51,886	73	48	4	125
1943	80,192	32	55	-	87
1944	70,930	46	66	6	118
1945	49,247	77	91	3	171
1946	73,524	65	44	1	110
1947	36,378	122	23	4	149
1948	71,435	-	79	-	79
1949	49,983	66	61	3	130
1950	69,358	46	50	-	96
1951	70,505	31	59	-	90
1952	59,084	42	46	-	88
1953	62,958	8	57	-	65
1954	61,214	25	39	1	65
1955	41,025	59	53	15	127
1956	54,310	39	58	-	97
1957	52,736	63	41	1	105
1958	55,825	40	147	1	85
1959	60,508		record ends		
1960	46,583				
1961	44,204				
1962	49,708				

wks=heavy and light repairs at main works
shed=shed repairs and examinations
n/req= not required

Total Recorded Mileage 1,492,619
Withdrawn. Curiously, no note made, but the tender 'attached to 46223' is recorded instead, 'withdrawn period ending 5/10/63'. 46223 was indeed withdrawn in October that year.
Cut up Crewe Works 10/63

Repairs BR

[Dates in first column are from out of traffic to return to traffic; the two 'mileage' figures represent, firstly the miles accumulated since the previous General or Intermediate and secondly (the generally lower figure) the miles run up from January 1st of the year of shopping. All are recorded as taking place at Crewe unless otherwise noted. StR=St Rollox]

Dates	Weekdays Waiting	Weekdays On Works	Mileage	'Jan 1' Mileage
23/7/51-28/8/51**HI**	7	24	92,743	36,636
22/8/52-10/10/52**HG**	5	37	78,223	44,097
23/12/53-2/2/54**HI**	6	27	77,688	nil
31/5/54-5/6/54**NC***	-	(StR)	-	-
18/2/55-18/2/55**NC**	-	(StR)	-	-
27/4/55-28/4/55**NC**	-	(StR)	-	-
17/6/55-25/8/55**HG**	27	32	80,715	19,501
27/8/56-11/10/56**LC***	4	35	62,560	41,036
8/4/57-17/5/57**HI**	3	31	92,519	16,246
9/11/57-14/12/57**LC**	5	26	35,288	51,534
30/9/58-15/11/58**HI**	11	29	85,536	49,014
26/4/60-2/7/60**HG**	30	28	80,007	12,752
22/8/60-19/11/60**LC**	4	73	-	-
15/11/61-5/1/62**HI**	14	28	78,035	44,204

*****=*'(EO)' - 'Engine Only'*

Sheds

Camden	3/7/37
Polmadie (loan)	25/11/39
Polmadie	30/12/39

Tenders

No	Fitted
9706	28/6/37
9748	6/5/46

Boilers

Fitted	No.	From
17/4/40	9939	6222
1/11/41	9938	6221
30/5/42	10642	new
13/7/45	10301	6232
5/12/47	10297	6233
14/4/50	10292	6220
10/10/52	10297	-
25/8/55	9940	-
2/7/60	10299	-

No record after this date

46223 PRINCESS ALICE on The Royal Scot at Beattock, 26 July 1952. With this sort of view, one would hardly demur from any suggestion that the Coronations were without equal when it came power. Photograph J. Robertson, B.P. Hoper Collection.

You'll Remember those Black and White Days...

46224 PRINCESS ALEXANDRA at Glasgow Central, waiting to depart with The Royal Scot in April 1954. The way the 'big 'uns' were crewed was very different, according to the shed which operated them. In BR days, for instance, Crewe North men in the famous 'Perth Link' worked the whole of the 296 miles to Perth, lodging with their engines before returning. Polmadie men came to Crewe but Perth men, on the other hand, never proceeded south of Carlisle. Photograph J. Robertson, B.P. Hoper Collection.

46224 PRINCESS ALEXANDRA

Built Crewe 13/7/37, cost £10,095 (engine), £1,546 (tender)
Built streamlined, casing removed 27/6/46
Renumbered 6224 to 46224 week ending 8/5/48

Repairs LMS

26/8/37-1/9/37**LO**	10/9/43-16/10/43**HG**
26/1/38-10/2/38**LO**	10/7/44-17/8/44**LS**
2/9/38-22/9/38**LS**	17/2/45-28/3/45**HG**
10/3/39-27/3/39**LO**	14/5/46-27/6/46**HS**
14/7/39-31/7/39**LS**	4/10/47-22/11/47**HS**
25/4/40-29/5/40**HG**	9/3/48-3/5/48**HG**
10/9/40-5/11/40**HO**	19/5/48-31/5/48 **'NIL'**
29/3/41-19/4/41**HS**	21/11/48-21/12/48**LO**
24/3/42-14/4/42**LS**	8/6/49-8/8/49**LI**
15/3/43-15/4/43**LS**	29/6/50-26/8/50**HG**

LMS 'Summary' *(this became 'Annual Statistics' from 1951)*

Year	Mileage	Weekdays out of service			
		wks	shed	n/req	total
1937	31,149	6	19	11	36
1938	63,289	32	63	19	114
1939	60,093	30	55	24	109
1940	63,147	79	53	26	158
1941	67,276	19	52	8	81
1942	75,354	19	64	-	83
1943	63,994	60	51	3	114
1944	68,979	34	59	6	99
1945	70,768	34	64	-	98
1946	57,484	39	86	5	130
1947	53,445	43	65	-	108
1948	55,145	82	43	2	127
1949	67,583	53	46	2	101
1950	60,169	59	38	1	98
1951	75,695	41	55	-	96
1952	57,162	42	53	1	96
1953	68,535	33	36	2	71
1954	51,486	34	52	-	86
1955	55,008	-	80	12	92
1956	44,865	67	61	-	128
1957	47,772	50	48	2	100
1958	66,379		*record ends*		
1959	41,947				
1960	46,098				
1961	34,769				
1962	42,899				

wks=heavy and light repairs at main works
shed=shed repairs and examinations
n/req= not required

Total Recorded Mileage 1,490,488
Withdrawn week ending 19/10/63
Cut up Crewe Works 10/63

Repairs BR

[Dates in first column are from out of traffic to return to traffic; the two 'mileage' figures represent, firstly the miles accumulated since the previous General or Intermediate and secondly (the generally lower figure) the miles run up from January 1st of the year of shopping. All are recorded as taking place at Crewe unless otherwise noted. StR=St Rollox]

Dates	Weekdays Waiting	Weekdays On Works	Mileage	'Jan 1' Mileage
5/9/50-15/9/50**NC**	-	9	404	31,573
8/3/51-25/4/51**HI**	18	23	47,646	18,646
7/4/52-20/5/52**HG**	3	34	70,717	13,668
26/5/52-31/5/52**NC**	-	5	460	14,128
12/5/53-19/6/53**HI**	8	25	71,083	27,589
14/9/54-23/10/54**HI**	7	27	81,198	40,252
4/5/54-4/5/54**NC**	-	1(StR)	61,592	20,646
1/2/56-14/3/56**LI**	10	26	71,014	4,559
16/5/56-16/5/56**NC**	-	1(StR)	5,370	9,929
8/10/56-10/11/56**LC***	9	20	32,472	37,031
14/11/56-16/11/56**NC***	-	2	32,567	37,126
27/7/57-24/9/57**HG**	14	36	73,626	32,419
3/4/59-20/5/59**LI**	11	29	93,262	12,320
5/10/59-4/12/59**LC***	22	30	25,640	37,709
10/3/60-7/5/60**LI**	17	32	43,358	13,731
4/11/61-3/1/61**HC***	14	35	32,367	46,098
25/10/61-5/1/62**HG**	22	38	67,136	34,769

*='(EO)' - Engine Only

Sheds

Polmadie	30/12/39

Tenders

No	Fitted
9707	13/7/37
9748	14/8/45
9706	6/5/46

Boilers

Fitted	No.	From
29/5/40	9937	6220
5/11/40	10300	6228
16/10/43	10289	6237
28/3/45	10290	6225
27/6/46	10305	6229
3/5/48	10301	6223
26/8/50	10303	6250
20/5/52	10643	-
23/10/54	10293	-
24/9/57	9941	-
6/1/62	10288	-

That splendid outline. 46224 PRINCESS ALEXANDRA at Camden in the early 1950s. The Coronations suffered few mishaps but by an extraordinary and infernal coincidence PRINCESS ALEXANDRA suffered two of the worst; moreover both were that most singular and destructive 'self-inflicted' accident rare since the early days of railways—a form of boiler explosion. With wartime staff shortages, 6224 on a London train was put into the hands of an inexperienced 'passed' crew at Glasgow Central on 10 September 1940. They had never worked anything the size of this and through lack of familiarity with the engine and the work, managed to expose the firebox crown on the climb to Craigenhill. There was a violent explosion and the Fireman scalded, to death. The works visit for repairs dates from the same day, 10 September. In a bizarre coincidence, the engine sustained another crown collapse, on 5 March 1948, at Lamington only twelve miles or so from the scene of the first disaster. This time it was the Driver who was killed, despite his long experience of the Coronations. 6224 went to Crewe for repair once again, four days later, emerging in May as 46224. Photograph Alec Swain, B.P.Hoper Collection.

46225 DUCHESS OF GLOUCESTER, in blue at Polmadie with The Mid-Day Scot, 9 May 1953. The train was a prime Crewe North job, out and home and the only one in the Perth Link in which the crew saw daylight from the footplate in the winter months. Men either stayed in the Perth Link year after year, loving it, or they heartily detested it, and skipped it all together. For this reason it was not part of the 'normal' progression through the links at Crewe—see Allan Baker and Gavin Morrison's *Crewe Sheds*, Ian Allan, 1988 and a wonderful read. Photograph J. Robertson, B.P. Hoper Collection.

A blue DUCHESS OF GLOUCESTER, newly painted about 1950. A curious feature is (what looks to be) something akin to the bracket of the old Stone-Deuta speed indicator. The story is well known of the prodigious output recorded with 46225 on the Rugby Test Plant in the 1950s, and the general conclusion was that the locomotives were really working within the capabilities of the single Fireman, rather than the boiler... Photograph J. Robertson, B.P. Hoper Collection.

LMS 'Summary' (this became 'Annual Statistics' from 1951)

Year	Mileage	wks	shed	n/req	total
		Weekdays out of service			
1938	53,126	18	24	2	44
1939	78,386	15	86	11	112
1940	61,957	34	50	17	101
1941	79,372	17	47	1	65
1942	70,079	34	48	-	82
1943	78,942	21	53	1	75
1944	63,028	80	51	-	131
1945	69,800	40	110	-	150
1946	82,352	27	40	4	71
1947	70,803	36	50	-	86
1948	68,077	25	70	3	98
1949	76,794	29	42	5	76
1950	55,323	74	49	6	129
1951	68,633	37	44	-	81
1952	78,600	35	61	-	96
1953	62,529	77	41	2	120
1954	56,349	43	63	-	106
1955	54,215#	15	26	109	150
1956	64,961	19	55	-	74
1957	70,988	38	32	-	70
1958	66,869	47	51	-	98
1959	62,154		*record ends*		
1960	77,457				
1961	41,982				
1962	58,491				
1963	40,757				
1964	35,000##				

'includes miles run at Rugby Test Station'
'estimate'
wks=heavy and light repairs at main works
shed=shed repairs and examinations
n/req= not required

Total Recorded Mileage 1,609,518
Withdrawn week ending 12/9/64
Cut up West of Scotland
Shipbreaking Co. Troon 12/64

46225 DUCHESS OF GLOUCESTER

Built Crewe 11/5/38, cost £10,136 (tender £1,601)
Built streamlined, casing removed 24/3/47
Renumbered 6225 to 46225 week ending 19/6/48

Repairs BR

[Dates in first column are from out of traffic to return to traffic; the two 'mileage' figures represent, firstly the miles accumulated since the previous General or Intermediate and secondly (the generally lower figure) the miles run up from January 1st of the year of shopping. All are recorded as taking place at Crewe unless otherwise noted. StR=St Rollox]

Dates	Weekdays Waiting	Weekdays On Works	Mileage	'Jan 1' Mileage
31/3/50-21/4/50**LC**	-	17	198	4,787
13/12/50-21/1/51**LC**	3	22	50,734	55,323
22/9/51-24/10/51**HI**	6	21	105,206	54,472
26/3/52-4/4/52**NC***	3	5	33,613	19,452
18/5/52-28/6/52**LI**	7	28	46,580	32,419
24/1/53-21/3/53**HG**	3	46	49,283	3,102
25/3/53-26/3/53**NC***	-	1	140	3,242
9/10/53-10/11/53**LC***	9	18	48,507	51,609
12/1/54-16/1/54**NC***	3	1	62,559	3,132
11/11/54-20/1/55**HG**	3	55	115,776	56,349
23/6/55-1/7/55**NC***	1	6	10,339	10,339
17/2/56-10/3/56**HI**	2	17	65,762	11,547
9/5/56-18/5/56**NC***	-	8	5,409	16,956
16/4/57-18/4/57**NC***	-	2	76,141	22,727
15/8/57-28/9/57**HI**	5	33	102,826	49,412
13/6/58-7/8/58**HG**	6	41	56,532	34,956
6/11/59-1/1/60**LI**	12	34	93,836	61,923
11/3/60-14/4/60**LC***	16	13	20,436	20,205
2/8/61-9/10/61**HG**	6	52	106,356	28,668

*=‘(EO)’ - ‘Engine Only’

Sheds

Camden	21/5/38
Holyhead	21/10/39
Crewe North	6/4/40
Polmadie (loan)	11/5/40
Crewe North	15/6/46
Camden	22/5/43
Crewe North	12/10/46
Camden	11/10/47
Crewe North	1/10/49
Camden	5/7/52
Crewe North	20/9/52
Rugby Test Station	22/1/55
Crewe North	4/6/55
Carlisle Upperby	27/6/59
Stored 2/1/64 - 27/1/64	

Tenders

No	Fitted
9743	11/5/38
9749	9/8/45
9799	11/3/49

Boilers

Fitted	No.	From
27/8/40	10302	6331
22/8/42	10290	6238
22/9/44	10291	6239
24/3/47	10638	6248
28/3/50	10642	-
21/3/53	12472	-
20/1/55	10645	-
7/8/58	10301	-
7/10/61	10693	-

No record after this date

Repairs LMS

12/8/38-1/9/38**LO**	16/5/44-22/7/44**HG**
18/4/39-4/5/39**LS**	10/2/45-28/3/45**HS**
19/7/40-29/8/40**HG**	6/3/46-5/4/46**LS**
23/9/41-11/10/41**LS**	11/2/47-24/3/47**HG**
7/3/42-21/3/42**LO**	26/10/47-4/11/47**NC**
30/7/42-22/8/42**HG**	22/5/48-19/6/48**LS**
1/6/43-24/6/43**HS**	7/2/49-11/3/49**HI**
15/3/44-7/4/44**HS**	11/6/49-16/6/49**NC**
	7/2/50-28/3/50**HG**

46225 DUCHESS OF GLOUCESTER leaving Rugby with the 1.30pm Euston - Perth on 22 July 1961. As a streamliner, 6225 had a part in one of the nastier accidents involving the Coronations, derailing with the 'Services sleeper' at Mossband on 15 May 1944, and killing three passengers. Photograph Michael Mensing.

Rain-streaked 46226 DUCHESS OF NORFOLK, luxuriating in that sublime form which, even one raised on the glories of the East Coast has to concede, was simply breathtaking. This is the modern open roundhouse at Carlisle Upperby about 1950. Photograph J. Robertson, B.P. Hoper Collection.

46226 DUCHESS OF NORFOLK in work-stained glory, about 1955, at Polmadie. The Duchesses proper (though the name was frequently accorded to the class as a whole) were the ten engines built in 1938, the first five streamlined, the second not so. Maybe the LMS ran out of suitably exalted nobility, though there were surely plenty more; there was no Duchess of York for instance, and no Duchess of Bedford for that matter. Photograph J. Robertson, B.P. Hoper Collection.

LMS 'Summary' *(this became 'Annual Statistics' from 1951)*

Year	Mileage	Weekdays out of service			
		wks	shed	n/req	total
1938	61,341	-	46	1	47
1939	69,456	28	53	13	108#
1940	65,229	46	63	5	114
1941	53,227	69	50	-	119
1942	71,862	37	39	-	76
1943	73,235	21	57	-	78
1944	72,909	45	52	-	97
1945	71,171	54	45	2	101
1946	73,777	28	70	2	100
1947	51,342	46	83	7	136
1948	53,942	57	58	3	118
1949	70,735	41	45	3	89
1950	67,085	26	53	2	81
1951	61,013	36	77	1	114
1952	65,765	22	55	6	83
1953	65,795	-	85	8	93
1954	63,955	44	49	4	97
1955	63,953	27	57	9	93
1956	81,619	-	57	8	65
1957	60,997	36	62	11	109
1958	63,489	38	64	11	113
1959	75,052				

#incudes 14 days 'stored serviceable'
wks=heavy and light repairs at main works
shed=shed repairs and examinations
n/req= not required

Total Recorded Mileage 1,456,949
Withdrawn week ending 12/9/64
Cut up West of Scotland
Shipbreaking Co. Troon 2/65

6226 DUCHESS OF NORFOLK at what looks to be Camden. The *art deco* lamps are a delight and the sandbox caps are prominent in this low angle light, set flush with the casing. The works plate, in the region of the middle driving wheel (moved to a hardly visible site below a step on the front framing after the casing was removed—see the previous picture of 46226 with its Crewe plate tucked away) is very apparent. In this light the unsightly raised parts of the casing, most noticeably over the cylinders, are also clearly picked out—they recalled, unfortunately, the half-hearted GWR 'smoothed out' school of streamlining. Photograph P. Ransome Wallis.

46226 DUCHESS OF NORFOLK

Built Crewe 23/5/38 cost £9,372 (engine), £1,570 (tender)
Built streamlined, casing removed 27/11/48
Renumbered 6226 to 42226 week ending 25/9/48

Repairs BR

[Dates in first column are from out of traffic to return to traffic; the two 'mileage' figures represent, firstly the miles accumulated since the previous General or Intermediate and secondly (the generally lower figure) the miles run up from January 1st of the year of shopping. All are recorded as taking place at Crewe unless otherwise noted. StR=St Rollox]

Dates	Weekdays Waiting	Weekdays On Works	Mileage	'Jan 1' Mileage
20/4/51-1/6/51**HG**	3	33	59,870	14,952
12/9/52-8/10/52**LI**	2	20	96,668	50,607
23/3/54-14/5/54**HG**	2	42	95,791	14,838
12/10/55-12/11/55**HI**	4	23	105,754	56,637
28/3/57-10/5/57**HG**	9	27	103.098	14,163
23/10/57-6/11/57**NC***	8	4	37,959	52,122
15/10/58-28/11/58**H**	6	32	103,337	56,503
24/3/60-18/6/60**HG**	15	58	93,967	11,929

record ends
*='(EO)' - 'Engine Only'

Sheds

Camden	28/5/38
Speke Jct	16/9/39
Holyhead	21/10/39
Camden	9/12/39
Crewe	6/4/40
Camden	22/5/43
Carlisle Upperby	12/10/46
Camden (loan)	23/6/51
Camden	7/7/51
Carlisle Upperby	15/9/51
Edge Hill	14/11/53
Carlisle Upperby	12/12/53
Edge Hill	22/1/55
Carlisle	5/3/55
Crewe North	29/9/56
Carlisle Upperby	20/10/56

Stored 16/9/39 - 2/10/39

Tenders

No	Fitted
9744	23/5/38

Boilers

Fitted	No.	From
23/5/38	10298	new
14/9/40	9941	6224
3/1/42	9940	6228
25/7/42	10304	6233
20/10/45	10302	6230
23/9/48	9939	6235
1/6/51	10306	46245
14/5/54	10296	-
10/5/57	10638	-
18/6/60	10640	-

No record after this date

Repairs LMS

2/1/39-17/1/39**LO**	17/4/44-12/5/44**LS**
4/5/39-19/5/39**LS**	5/12/44-30/1/45**LS**
14/5/40-24/5/40**TRO**	19/9/45-20/10/45**HG**
5/8/40-14/9/40**HG**	30/7/46-30/8/46**HS**
12/4/41-8/3/41**LO**	15/10/47-21/11/47**LS**
28/8/41-30/9/41**LS**	2/12/47-16/12/47**NC**
6/12/41-3/1/42**HO**	20/7/48-23/9/48**HG**
20/6/42-25/7/42**HG**	4/7/49-10/8/49**LI**
10/5/43-2/6/43**HS**	15/4/50-16/5/50**HI**

You'll Remember those Black and White Days...

LMS 'Summary' (this became 'Annual Statistics' from 1951)

Year	Mileage	Weekdays out of service			
		wks	shed	n/req	total
1938	58,007	-	31	1	32
1939	77,944	26	51	23	100
1940	72,530	31	43	28	102
1941	73.539	2	72	-	74
1942	57,222	91	47	-	138
1943	61,277	69	67	-	136
1944	77,781	36	37	-	73
1945	73,925	41	77	2	120
1946	72,472	64	32	2	98
1947	63,260	67	21	1	89
1948	51,376	45	79	1	125
1949	57,912	28	75	2	105
1950	49,667	50	69	-	119
1951	62,062	-	91	1	92
1952	48,593	66	70	3	139
1953	58,038	53	58	2	113
1954	49,119	31	66	-	97
1955	51,452	25	65	9	103
1956	39,526	79	60	1	140
1957	39,151	76	50	-	126
1958	56,511	33	57	-	90
1959	55,830			record ends	
1960	50,100				
1961	44,175				
1962	42,170				

wks=heavy and light repairs at main works
shed=shed repairs and examinations
n/req= not required

Total Recorded Mileage 1,443,639
Withdrawn week ending 29/12/62
Cut up Crewe Works 11/63

Repairs LMS

16/1/39-31/1/39**LO**	12/9/44-4/10/44**LS**
15/5/39-27/5/39**LS**	6/7/45-22/8/45**HG**
22/11/40-31/12/40**HG**	12/1/46-13/2/46**LO**
29/12/41-31/1/42**LS**	16/7/46-26/8/46**HS**
20/6/42-17/7/42**LO**	22/2/47-26/3/47**HO**
5/11/42-17/12/42**HG**	11/8/47-24/9/47**LS**
26/6/43-27/7/43**LO**	5/3/48-6/4/48**LO**
25/10/43-11/12/43**LS**	13/4/48-3/5/48**NC**
14/3/44-31/3/44**LO**	14/3/49-14/4/49**LI**
	26/6/50-23/8/50**HG**

46227 DUCHESS OF DEVONSHIRE

Built Crewe 7/6/38, cost £9,732 (engine), £1,570 (tender)
Built streamlined, casing removed 26/8/46
Renumbered 6227 to 46227 week ending 8/5/48

Repairs BR

[Dates in first column are from out of traffic to return to traffic; the two 'mileage' figures represent, firstly the miles accumulated since the previous General or Intermediate and secondly (the generally lower figure) the miles run up from January 1st of the year of shopping. All are recorded as taking place at Crewe unless otherwise noted. StR=St Rollox]

Dates	Weekdays Waiting	Weekdays On Works	Mileage	'Jan 1' Mileage
5/2/52-10/3/52**HI**	2	27	90,525	5,526
29/9/52-11/11/52**LC***	12	25	35,589	41,115
16/2/53-18/4/53**'GEN'**	10	43	51,982	8,915
5/2/54-13/3/54**LC***	8	23	54,625	5,502
18/5/54-18/5/54**NC***	-(StR)	-	57,329	8,206
21/5/55-19/2/55**HI**	3	22	102,246	4,004
23/3/56-24/3/56**NC**	-(StR)	-	59,944	12,236
16/6/56-11/8/56**HG**	7	41	72,097	24,389
24/10/56-29/11/56**LC***	11	20	9,600	33,990
24/6/57-17/8/57**LC***	2	45	37,947	22,366
13/11/57-8/2/58**LI**	32	41	54,288	38,707
16/2/59-4/4/59**LI**	7	33	64,216	7,705
16/3/60-21/5/60**HI**	18	38	57,061	8,936
1/3/61-18/5/61**HG**	29	37	50,615	9,451

record ends
*='(EO)' - 'Engine Only'

Sheds

Camden	18/6/38
Holyhead	21/10/39
Crewe	6/4/40
Camden	22/5/43
Carlisle Upperby	12/10/46
Camden	24/5/47
Crewe North	21/6/47
Polmadie (loan)	12/6/48
Polmadie	14/8/48

Tenders

No	Fitted
9745	7/6/38

Boilers

Fitted	No.	From
31/12/40	10298	6226
17/12/42	10288	6236
22/8/45	10642	6223
26/3/47	10299	6235
23/8/50	10638	6225
18/4/53	10637	-
11/8/56	10298	-
18/5/61	9938	-

No record after this date

46227 DUCHESS OF DEVONSHIRE at Polmadie, 14 April 1962. The engine is in BR green, which it got in 1953. BR fitments by this time are the prominent AWS, revealed by the guard plate behind the screw coupling and the battery box in front of the cab and the cylindrical vacuum reservoir on the footplating (there was a smaller subsidiary one on the other side). Photograph James Stevenson.

46228 DUCHESS OF RUTLAND, wreathed (above and left) in its own outpourings, firstly on leaving Rugby and secondly in more dignified pose, near Tamworth with the down Royal Scot, Sunday 21 June 1959. The lower picture demonstrates the worth of those smoke deflectors, lifting the exhaust high and free off the top of the boiler and away from the cab windows. Photographs B.P. Hoper Collection and (below) Michael Mensing.

LMS 'Summary' (this became 'Annual Statistics' from 1951)

Year	Mileage	Weekdays out of service			
		works	shed	n/req	total
1938	52,124	-	27	4	31
1939	78,276	26	43	17	107#
1940	53,082	42	61	35	138
1941	70,920	66	34	-	100
1942	58,100	59	57	1	117
1943	64,908	25	73	-	98
1944	72,918	31	59	-	90
1945	56,651	67	67	1	135
1946	79,242	22	68	1	91
1947	41,377	103	54	5	162
1948	70,947	44	45	1	89
1949	36,865	115	64	3	182
1950	56,737	82	31	3	116
1951	71,396	20	67	1	88
1952	67,659	5	61	9	75
1953	43,428	88	52	11	151
1954	68,661	-	62	9	71
1955	70,643	37	47	3	87
1956	67,905	23	71	11	105
1957	69,981	15	57	6	78
1958	71,862	37	43	1	81
1959	70,412			record ends	

# 'includes 11 days stored serviceable'
works=heavy and light repairs at main works
shed=shed repairs and examinations
n/req= not required

Total Recorded Mileage 1,337,772
Withdrawn week ending 12/9/64
Cut up J.Cashmore, Great Bridge, 12/64

Repairs LMS

4/2/39-22/2/39**LO**	14/8/44-25/8/44**LO**
19/6/39-29/6/39**LS**	14/3/45-14/4/45**HS**
29/7/40-31/8/40**HG**	14/8/45-27/9/45**LO**
5/9/40-17/9/40**LO**	26/5/46-20/6/46**LS**
28/12/40-9/1/41**LO**	19/6/47-16/10/47**HG**
20/2/41-18/3/41**LO**	5/6/48-26/7/48**LO**
26/6/41-2/8/41**HO**	4/1/49-28/1/49**LI**
15/1/42-21/2/42**LS**	15/3/49-1/7/49**HC**
26/11/42-2/1/43**HS**	31/1/50-7/3/50**LC**
4/8/43-25/8/43**LO**	9/5/50-27/5/50**NC**
24/4/44-16/5/44**HG**	21/8/50-2/10/50**HG**

46228 DUCHESS OF RUTLAND

Built Crewe 17/6/38, cost £9,732 (engine), £1,601(tender)
Built streamlined, casing removed 16/10/47
Renumbered 6228 to 46228 week ending 31/7/48

Repairs BR
[Dates in first column are from out of traffic to return to traffic; the two 'mileage' figures represent, firstly the miles accumulated since the previous General or Intermediate and secondly (the generally lower figure) the miles run up from January 1st of the year of shopping. All are recorded as taking place at Crewe unless otherwise noted. StR=St Rollox]

Dates	Weekdays Waiting	Weekdays On Works	Mileage	'Jan 1' Mileage
5/12/51-5/1/51**LI**	4	21	90,497	71,396
3/1/53-27/2/53**HG**	15	32	68,403	444
9/3/53-27/3/53**HC***	-	16	289	733
11/11/53-10/12/53**HC***	8	17	39,777	40,221
23/4/55-6/6/55**HG**	3	34	135,099	23,454
1/12/56-17/1/57**HI**	13	25	115,094	67,905
29/9/57-2/10/57**NC***	-	2	49,759	49,759
9/5/58-21/6/58**HI**	2	35	99,198	29,217
3/7/59-2/9/59**HG**	21	31	86,101	43,456
29/12/60-18/2/61**LI**	12	32	106,359	127

record ends
*='(EO)' - 'Engine Only'

Sheds

Camden	18/6/38
Longsight	16/9/39
Rugby	30/9/39
Holyhead	21/10/39
Crewe	6/4/40
Camden	22/5/43
Carlisle Upperby	12/10/46
Camden	7/7/51
Carlisle Upperby	15/9/51
Edge Hill	5/6/54
Carlisle Upperby	19/6/54
Edge Hill	25/9/54
Carlisle Upperby	16/10/54
Crewe North	21/9/57
Carlisle Upperby	20/6/59

Stored 15/9/39 to 21/9/39, 27/9/39 to 2/10/39, 24/9/63 to 12/12/63

Tenders

No	Fitted
9746	17/6/38

Boilers

Fitted	No.	From
31/8/40	9940	6223
2/8/41	9937	6224
16/5/44	10295	6243
16/10/47	9941	6239
2/10/50	10693	6239
27/2/53	10694	-
6/6/55	10288	-
2/9/59	10291	-

No record after this date

A blaze of red and gold, 6228 DUCHESS OF RUTLAND at Tring summit with the up Royal Scot, just before the Second World War. Photograph C.R.L. Coles.

LMS 'Summary' (this became 'Annual Statistics' from 1951)

Year	Mileage	Weekdays out of service			
		wks	shed	n/req	total
1938	15,131	20	20	-	40
1939	USA	6	1	-	7
1940	USA	-	-	-	-
1941	USA	-	-	-	-
1942	61,368	43	23	1	67
1943	72,667	59	33	-	92
1944	79,805	22	45	1	68
1945	81,223	22	142	3	167
1946	77,910	43	63	2	108
1947	55,603	78	41	-	119
1948	78,285	12	63	1	76
1949	66,107	27	76	5	108
1950	78,954	33	17	11	61
1951	75,303	42	27	-	69
1952	81,249	34	60	-	94
1953	78,739	39	59	-	98
1954	73,038	78	35	-	113
1955	72,867	16	88	9	113
1956	87,208	40	59	-	99
1957	83,150	35	55	-	90
1958	74,833	50	58	-	108
1959	90,994			record ends	
1960	55,058				
1961	47,990				
1962	27,758				
1963	16,596				

wks=heavy and light repairs at main works
shed=shed repairs and examinations
n/req= not required

Total Recorded Mileage 1,454,892
Withdrawn week ending 15/2/64
Preserved at Butlins, then NRM

Repairs LMS
9/12/38-7/1/39**LO**
23/2/42-18/3/42**LO**
USA
17/10/42-11/11/42**LS**
12/3/43-20/4/43**LO**
28/8/43-25/9/43**HG**
30/10/44-23/11/44**LS**
4/12/45-25/1/46**HG**
15/10/46-6/11/46**LS**
24/4/47-19/5/47**LO**
23/10/47-10/1/48**HG**
3/4/48-9/4/48**NC**
29/6/48-1/7/48 **'Nil'**
25/5/49-24/6/49**LI**

46229 DUCHESS OF HAMILTON

Built Crewe 7/9/38, cost £9,732 (engine), £1,570 (tender)
Built streamlined, casing removed 10/1/48
Renumbered and renamed 6220 CORONATION for America - shipped 20/1/39
Returned to Traffic 18/3/42
Renumbered 6229 during repairs completed 20/4/43
Renumbered 6229 to 46229 week ending 3/7/48

Repairs BR
[Dates in first column are from out of traffic to return to traffic; the two 'mileage' figures represent, firstly the miles accumulated since the previous General or Intermediate and secondly (the generally lower figure) the miles run up from January 1st of the year of shopping. All are recorded as taking place at Crewe unless otherwise noted. StR=St Rollox]

Dates	Weekdays Waiting	Weekdays On Works	Mileage	'Jan 1' Mileage
16/1/50-23/2/50**HG**	-	23	-	-
6/1/51-7/2/51**LI**	4	23	76,648	1,272
17/3/52-26/4/52**HG**	1	33	90,472	16,441
23/3/53-8/5/53**HI**	15	24	85,132	20,324
22/1/54-19/3/54**HG**	6	42	63,414	4,999
6/11/54-11/12/54**LC**	1	29	63,875	68,874
5/5/55-23/5/55**LC**	1	14	100,154	32,115
31/12/55-17/2/56**HG**	1	40	140,906	Nil
21/1/57-2/3/57**HI**	9	26	92,920	5,712
16/9/57-19/9/57**NC***	-	3	49,208	54,920
14/7/58-10/9/58**HI**	16	34	122,608	45,170
17/8/59-8/10/59**HG**	6	39	95,669	66,006
21/3/60-7/5/60**NC***	24	16	42,472	17,484
12/7/60-26/8/60**LC***	13	26	57,365	32,377
13/5/61-13/6/61**HI**	2	24	101,339	19,293

Record ends
*='(EO)' - 'Engine Only'

Sheds

Crewe North	10/9/38
Camden	15/5/43
Crewe North	21/6/47
Camden	24/4/48
Crewe North	1/10/49

Record ends, but was at Camden by 1954, and went to Edge Hill in 3/61 Stored 8/10/62 to we 2/2/63, 14/10/63 to 23/12/63, 30/12/63 to 10/2/64

Tenders

No	Fitted
9747	7/9/38
9802	22/11/45

Boilers

Fitted	No.	From
25/9/43	10305	6233
25/1/46	10298	6222
10/1/48	10645	6252
23/2/50	9938	6237
23/2/50	9938	-
26/4/52	10639	-
19/3/54	9939	-
17/2/56	10302	-
8/10/59	10297	-

Record ends

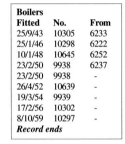

Camden's 46229 DUCHESS OF HAMILTON at Glasgow Central on 6 April 1955. It remained a 'Semi' until quite late and did not get a conventional smokebox until the early part of 1957. It has been famously restored of course, having the good luck to be bought by Billy Butlin, who came to Crewe to look at it himself. Photograph J. Robertson, B.P. Hoper Collection.

You'll Remember those Black and White Days...

46230 DUCHESS OF BUCCLEUCH

Built Crewe 27/6/38 cost £9,181(engine), £1,478 (tender)
Built without streamlining
Renumbered 6230 to 46230 week ending 15/5/48

LMS 'Summary' *(this became 'Annual Statistics' from 1951)*

Year	Mileage	Weekdays out of service			
		wks	shed	n/req	total
1938	47,941	-	31	1	32
1939	95,917	14	50	3	67
1940	80,816	28	44	13	85
1941	51,293	58	56	7	121
1942	68,121	15	63	7	85
1943	60,644	107	35	-	142
1944	65,576	39	74	6	119
1945	68,558	32	76	3	111
1946	72,551	19	68	-	87
1947	48,250	14	68	-	112
1948	63,048	47	60	1	108
1949	40,458	53	108	7	168
1950	65,824	65	21	-	86
1951	62,016	37	75	1	113
1952	60,796	57	49	-	106
1953	59,017	28	56	2	86
1954	56,434	-	80	-	80
1955	48,094	35	62	2	99
1956	59,992	-	74	3	77
1957	53,735	35	41	3	79
1958	42,654	38	93	2	133
1959	47,146	*record ends*			
1960	60,958				
1961	47,873				
1962	36,526				

wks=heavy and light repairs at main works
shed=shed repairs and examinations
n/req= not required

Total Recorded Mileage 1,464,238
Withdrawn week ending 9/11/63
Cut up Crewe Works 12/63

Repairs LMS

6/6/39-21/6/39**LS**	4/10/44-3/11/44**HS**
11/9/40-11/10/40**HS**	25/5/45-30/6/45**HG**
22/1/41-15/2/41**LO**	24/8/46-14/9/46**HS**
22/9/41-11/11/41**HG**	7/11/47-21/2/48**HG**
17/1/42-31/1/42**LO**	28/2/48-11/3/48**NC**
28/12/42-9/2/43**HS**	11/5/48-27/5/48**#**
1/9/43-15/10/43**LO**	#'*no repairs -*
20/11/43-11/1/44**LS**	*special painting for*
	liveries'

Repairs BR

[Dates in first column are from out of traffic to return to traffic; the two 'mileage' figures represent, firstly the miles accumulated since the previous General or Intermediate and secondly (the generally lower figure) the miles run up from January 1st of the year of shopping. All are recorded as taking place at Crewe unless otherwise noted. StR=St Rollox]

Dates	Weekdays Waiting	Weekdays On Works	Mileage	'Jan 1' Mileage
4/4/49-6/5/49**LI**	-	29	66,323	3,275
15/10/49-11/11/49**LC**	-	24	27,985	31,260
25/5/50-23/6/50**LI**	1	24	67,164	29,981
13/11/50-29/12/50**LC**	16	24	35,843	65,824
19/5/51-2/7/51**HI**	14	23	57,307	21,464
17/3/52-2/5/52**HG**	7	33	50,708	10,156
5/5/52-24/5/52**LC**	-	17	68	10,224
27/5/52-5/6/52**NC**	-	8	209	10,365
31/8/53-2/10/53**HI**	7	21	93,589	42,949
20/5/55-30/6/55**HG**	6	29	94,502	22,000
6/12/54**NC**	-(StR)	-	80,409	54,103
7/1/57-16/2/57**HI**	15	20	87,855	992
2/12/57-7/12/57**NC***	-	5	?	?
4/8/58-17/9/58**HI**	9	29	79,962	27,096
17/8/59-6/11/59**HC***	24	46	52,571	37,013
1/2/60-8/4/60**HG**	14	44	70,293	7,836
6/12/61-26/1/62**HG**	4	38	10,095	47,873
7/2/62-26/2/62**NC**	-	16	?	?
4/3/63**LC**			*record ends*	

*='(EO)' - 'Engine Only'

Sheds

Camden	7/6/38
Polmadie	10/2/40

Stored 3/12/62 to 29/12/62

Tenders

No	Fitted
9748	27/6/38
9707	14/8/45

Boilers

Fitted	No.	From
1/11/41	10299	6227
9/2/43	10302	6225
30/6/45	10641	6238
21/2/48	9940	6245
2/5/52	10305	-
30/6/55	10644	-
8/4/60	10302	-
27/1/62	10694	-

No record after this date

46230 DUCHESS OF BUCCLEUCH (its pronunciation prompted endless lineside argument) emerging from Drumlarig Tunnel with the 11am Carlisle to Glasgow St Enoch, on 10 July 1963. Photograph Michael Mensing.

Stirring view of 46230 DUCHESS OF BUCCLEUCH at Carlisle Citadel, 23 April 1953. The first of the engines built without streamlining, it had that hugely impressive curving crown of a smokebox from the first. Photograph James Stevenson.

46231 DUCHESS OF ATHOLL (in green and—because it was built so and did not get 'de-streamlined'—with sloping front to footplating) at Carlisle Kingmoor shed on 4 June 1954. The horizontal ROYAL SCOT headboard seems to have been introduced in June 1950 (but did not then have the tartan ground) and apparently was actually designed for the diesels, 10000-1 and 10201-3. The traditional curved headboard also remained in use. Certainly in BR days, the Polmadie engine hauling the Royal Scot came off at Carlisle, to be replaced by a Camden one; the Scottish engine later went back to Glasgow with the Down train. This led to the Polmadie engines having low mileages relative to Crewe and Camden examples. A noticeable external feature was the water feed valve and 'sieve' box on the tender underframe; located between the leading and middle tender axles, they fed the exhaust steam and live steam injectors—see, for instance, 46237 side on, page59. It was a modification (see 46231 without the equipment in the photograph opposite) which was developed under Ivatt with the Class 2 tanks and Moguls. The Record Cards make no mention of these fitments... Photograph A.G. Ellis, B.P. Hoper Collection.

You'll Remember those Black and White Days...

LMS 'Summary' (this became 'Annual Statistics' from 1951)

Year	Mileage	Weekdays out of service			
		wks	shed	n/req	total
1938	47,786	-	30	1	31
1939	88,155	22	63	1	86
1940	78,079	30	45	18	93
1941	64,075	31	54	19	104
1942	73,241	32	49	4	85
1943	61,556	86	39	1	126
1944	81,872	28	57	8	93
1945	69,932	65	40	2	107
1946	93,228	19	46	-	65
1947	39,336	92	69	1	162
1948	58,797	25	56	-	81
1949	61,850	42	56	1	99
1950	49,964	77	37	4	118
1951	69,906	29	62	1	92
1952	44,163	46	70	-	116
1953	40,053	84	70	2	156
1954	55,038	3	82	2	87
1955	48,953	76	19	14	109
1956	49,280	37	84	-	121
1957	56,898	25	41	2	68
1958	59,842	46	64	-	110
1959	56,412	record ends			
1960	54,673				
1961	44,221				
1962	25,129				

wks=heavy and light repairs at main works
shed=shed repairs and examinations
n/req= not required

Total Recorded Mileage 1,472,439
Withdrawn week ending 29/12/62
Cut up Crewe Works 11/63

Repairs LMS

30/6/39-25/7/39**LS**	1/8/46-22/8/46**LS**
29/4/40-1/6/40**HG**	22/4/47-30/5/47**LS**
7/6/41-12/7/41**LS**	14/8/47-21/8/47**NC**
19/6/42-25/7/42**HS**	15/10/47-20/12/47**HG**
1/1/43-17/2/43**LO**	8/5/48-25/5/48**#**
6/10/43-27/11/43**HG**	27/11/48-31/12/48**LO**
16/9/44-18/10/44**LS**	25/2/49-8/4/49**LI**
23/7/45-22/9/45**HG**	19/4/50-1/6/50**HI**
27/11/45-8/12/45**LO**	#'no repairs - special
	painting - new liveries'

46231 DUCHESS OF ATHOLL

Built Crewe 28/6/38 cost £9,181 (engine), £1,478 (tender)
Built without streamlining
Renumbered 6231 to 46231 week ending 29/5/48

Repairs BR

[Dates in first column are from out of traffic to return to traffic; the two 'mileage' figures represent, firstly the miles accumulated since the previous General or Intermediate and secondly (the generally lower figure) the miles run up from January 1st of the year of shopping. All are recorded as taking place at Crewe unless otherwise noted. StR=St Rollox]

Dates	Weekdays Waiting	Weekdays On Works	Mileage	'Jan 1' Mileage
15/11/50-19/1/51**HG**	12	42	32,404	49,964
29/1/51-15/2/51**NC**	-	15	467	467
27/2/51-12/3/51**NC**	-	11	1,203	1,203
27/6/52-20/8/52**LI**	4	42	12,557	22,651
25/3/53-5/5/53**LC**	16	19	33,973	12,461
8/7/53-11/7/53**LC**	1 (StR)	2	44,662	23,150
10/8/53-12/8/53**NC**	-	2	51,337	29,825
18/8/53-22/8/53**NC**	-	4	51,343	29,831
16/10/53-9/12/53**G**	14	32	58,477	36,965
19/8/54-19/8/54**NC**	- (StR)	1	39,342	36,254
20/12/54-23/12/54**LC***	2	1	57,793	54,705
28/2/55-16/4/55**LI**	12	28	67,088	8,962
16/11/55-16/11/55**NC***	- (StR)	1	39,345	48,307
21/11/55-6/1/56**LC***	14	24	39,991	48,953
26/1/56-17/2/56**NC***	-	19	40,288	297
12/12/56-26/1/57**LI**	14	23	89,271	49,280
18/11/57-18/11/57**NC**	- (StR)	1	-	-
24/12/57-28/12/57**LC***	-	4	56,989	56,898
31/3/58-23/5/58**G**	8	38	66,208	10,010
16/1/58-27/1/58**NC***	-	9	-	-
22/7/59-12/9/59**HI**	19	26	87,461	37,629
4/5/60-18/6/60**LC**	16	19	39,351	20,568
23/1/61-5/4/61**G**	-	62	76,195	2,739
11/1/62-2/3/62**LC**	13	30	-	-

record ends
***=*'(EO)' - 'Engine Only'*

Sheds

Camden	2/7/38
Polmadie (loan)	6/1/40
Polmadie	10/2/40
Stored 13/8/62 - 29/12/62	

Tenders

No	Fitted
9749	28/6/38
9812	23/1/45

Boilers

Fitted	No.	From
1/6/40	10639	new
27/11/43	10300	6224
2/9/45	10643	6236
20/12/47	10644	6249
19/1/51	9941	46228
9/12/53	10301	-
31/3/58	10287	-
No record after this date		

46231 DUCHESS OF ATHOLL with the smokestacks of industrial Glasgow as backdrop, on the Polmadie turntable 14 July 1948. 46231 was also involved in an accident, the terrible Ecclefechan collision of 21 July 1945. The train ran through signals and both Driver and Fireman were killed. Photograph James Stevenson.

46232 DUCHESS OF MONTROSE

Built Crewe 1/7/38, cost £9,181(engine), £1,478 (tender)
Built without streamlining
Renumbered 6232 to 46232 week ending 8/5/48

46232 DUCHESS OF MONTROSE restarts the 9.05am Blackpool to Dundee West relief from Beattock station, after summoning up a 2-6-4T at the rear as banker, on 29 July 1961. Photograph W.A.C. Smith.

Repairs BR

[Dates in first column are from out of traffic to return to traffic; the two 'mileage' figures represent, firstly the miles accumulated since the previous General or Intermediate and secondly (the generally lower figure) the miles run up from January 1st of the year of shopping. All are recorded as taking place at Crewe unless otherwise noted. StR=St Rollox]

Dates	Weekdays Waiting	Weekdays On Works	Mileage	'Jan 1' Mileage
20/6/49-23/8/49**HI**	-	56	69,030	24,442
28/9/50-9/11/50**HI**	7	29	72,944	45,041
7/4/51-19/5/51**LC**	16	20	37,658	27,068
24/9/51-17/11/51**HG**	15	32	61,462	50,872
18/9/52-17/10/52**HI**	4	21	63,160	54,161
10/4/53-20/5/53**LC**	11	23	34,156	18,814
6/1/54-10/2/54**HI**	10	20	76,114	896
11/11/54-5/2/55**'Gen'**	11	61	50,143	51,039
12/3/56-13/4/56**HI**	2	26	61,827	8,479
5/1/57-22/2/57**'Gen'**	16	25	47,695	123
11/12/57**NC***	-	2	-	-
3/3/58-12/4/58**HI**	6	28	59,861	8,665
26/1/59-14/3/59**LI**	8	33	53,794	6,428
19/10/59-5/12/59**LC**	15	26	37,993	44,277
18/8/60-28/10/60**HG**	7	54	90,428	49,520
3/11/60-19/11/60**LC***	-	13	90,428	-
17/5/61-28/6/61**LC***	10	26	27,728	21,492

record ends
*='(EO)' - 'Engine Only'

Sheds

Camden	2/7/38
Polmadie (loan)	6/1/40
Polmadie	10/2/40

Stored 13/8/62-29/12/62

Tenders

No	Fitted
9750	1/7/38

Boilers

Fitted	No.	From
4/9/40	10640	new
21/1/43	10301	6230
24/2/45	9937	6228
3/5/48	10298	6229
17/11/51	10644	-
5/2/55	12470	-
22/2/57	10290	-
28/10/60	10303	-

No record after this date

LMS 'Summary' *(this became 'Annual Statistics' from 1951)*

Year	Mileage	Weekdays out of service			
		wks	shed	n/req	
total					
1938	49,927	-	19	1	20
1939	93,258	13	51	2	66
1940	59,081	74	46	19	139
1941	59,991	71	45	12	128
1942	66,457	21	54	7	82
1943	57,349	55	45	2	102
1944	47,127	40	98	3	141
1945	71,076	61	50	4	115
1946	73,579	8	81	2	91
1947	44,634	69	74	1	144
1948	52,271	55	66	2	123
1949	52,345	56	64	-	120
1950	55,631	36	52	1	89
1951	59,871	83	57	-	140
1952	69,503	25	25	-	50
1953	59,876	34	51	1	86
1954	51,039	74	38	-	112
1955	53,348	28	57	14	99
1956	55,198	28	57	-	85
1957	51,346	41	62	-	103
1958	56,031	35	51	11	97
1959	47,336		*record ends*		
1960	55,756				
1961	51,666				
1962	27,252				

wks=heavy and light repairs at main works
shed=shed repairs and examinations
n/req= not required

Total Recorded Mileage 1,420,948
Withdrawn week ending 29/12/62
Cut up Crewe Works 11/63

46233 DUCHESS OF SUTHERLAND

Built Crewe 18/7/38, cost £9,181 (engine), £1,478 (tender)
Built without streamlining
Renumbered 6233 to 46233 week ending 2/10/48

St Rollox shed on 9 July 1955, and Crewe North's 46233 DUCHESS OF SUTHERLAND (presumably pinched by Perth for a Glasgow job) takes a draught of good Scottish water. Crewe North got its first Coronations in 1938, though until the big 70ft turntable went in during 1950 (in the aborted scheme to turn Crewe into a sort of 'super-shed') they had to proceed round the triangle Gresty Lane - Sorting Sidings North. Indeed so long were they that two other local triangles were barred to them! More rarely they used the 70ft turntable at Crewe South. Photograph J. Robertson, B.P. Hoper Collection.

LMS 'Summary' (this became 'Annual Statistics' from 1951)

Year	Mileage	Weekdays out of service			
		wks	shed	n/req	total
1938	46,599	2	20	1	23
1939	89,436	16	70	1	87
1940	82,750	14	71	-	85
1941	74,992	40	43	1	84
1942	54,163	50	63	1	114
1943	89,591	32	30	1	63
1944	60,844	68	41	1	110
1945	58,840	27	70	1	98
1946	68,480	37	38	-	75
1947	40,947	81	54	-	135
1948	67,934	54	36	1	91
1949	70,426	23	53	11	87
1950	65,291	32	38	12	82
1951	67,088	30	61	-	91
1952	74,461	60	41	-	101
1953	90,220	-	61	-	61
1954	76,890	21	39	2	62
1955	51,530	78	25	4	107
1956	61,490	62	46	2	110
1957	75,897	-	66	1	67
1958	63,439	40	39	1	80
1959	70,358		*record ends*		
1960	77,402				
1961	38,464				
1962	26,539				

wks=heavy and light repairs at main works
shed=shed repairs and examinations
n/req= not required

Total Recorded Mileage 1,644,071
Withdrawn week ending 8/2/64
Preserved at Bressingham

Repairs BR

[Dates in first column are from out of traffic to return to traffic; the two 'mileage' figures represent, firstly the miles accumulated since the previous General or Intermediate and secondly (the generally lower figure) the miles run up from January 1st of the year of shopping. All are recorded as taking place at Crewe unless otherwise noted. StR=St Rollox]

Dates	Weekdays Waiting	Weekdays On Works	Mileage	'Jan 1' Mileage
14/3/51-10/4/51**LC**	-	22	62,130	13,383
19/12/51-24/1/52**HI**	5	24	115,835	67,088
15/10/52-29/11/52**HG**	7	32	68,576	68,576
16/1/54-10/2/54**LI**	1	20	98,626	2,568
14/3/55-7/5/55**HI**	13	33	82,227	7,905
31/8/55-3/10/55**LC***	6	22	24,238	32,143
25/12/55-30/1/56**LC***	5	23	43,625	nil
25/10/56-8/12/56**HG**	9	29	101,032	57,407
12/10/57-23/10/57**NC***	9	2	62,823	58,740
24/2/58-12/4/58**HI**	2	38	92,569	12,589
1/8/59-26/9/59**HG**	4	44	101,590	50,741
18/1/61-21/2/61**HI**	5	24	98,848	1,929
10/7/61-24/8/61**LC***	14	25	22,363	23,997

record ends
*='(EO)' - 'Engine Only'

Sheds

Camden	23/7/38
Crewe North	20/5/44
Carlisle Upperby	14/6/58
Crewe North	20/9/58
Carlisle Upperby	2/4/60
Crewe North	23/4/60
Camden	30/4/60
Edge Hill	17/9/60

Stored 6/10/62 to we 2/2/63, 14/10/63 to 3/2/64

Tenders

No	Fitted
9751	18/7/38

Repairs LMS

10/7/39-27/7/39**LS**
1/7/40-16/7/40**LS**
5/2/41-8/3/41**HG**
5/6/41-18/6/41**TRO**
25/3/42-22/4/42**LS**
6/10/42-13/11/42**HS**
2/7/43-7/8/43**HG**
5/1/44-10/2/44**LO**
16/5/44-2/6/44**TRO**
12/10/44-3/11/44**LS**
18/4/45-19/5/45**HG**
15/2/46-7/3/46**LO**
3/8/46-24/8/46**HS**
26/7/47-28/10/47**HG**
3/11/47-14/11/47**#**
19/8/48-29/9/48**LS**
30/9/48-20/10/48**NC**
18/7/49-12/8/49**LI**
12/4/50-19/5/50**HG**
#'No Repair'

Boilers

Fitted	No.	From
8/3/41	10305	6234
7/8/43	10287	6235
19/5/45	10297	6234
28/10/47	10646	6250
19/5/50	10645	6229
29/11/52	10304	-
8/12/56	9937	-
26/9/59	10641	-

No record after this date

LMS 'Summary' *(this became 'Annual Statistics' from 1951)*

Year	Mileage	Weekdays out of service			
		works	shed	n/req	total
1938	38,595	-	19	1	20
1939	78,669	14	76	1	91
1940	82,915	47	62	3	112
1941	91,696	5	62	-	67
1942	57,407	70	39	1	110
1943	74,560	18	50	-	68
1944	51,062	23	74	3	100
1945	69,384	19	48	-	67
1946	61,580	64	31	-	95
1947	67,247	20	50	3	73
1948	50,133	71	46	-	117
1949	75,977	-	58	13	71
1950	64,625	61	34	6	101
1951	69,945	30	42	1	73
1952	76,968	35	58	-	93
1953	74,220	62	39	1	102
1954	71,379	32	36	1	69
1955	50,827	70	57	11	138
1956	89,179	-	38	2	40
1957	54,893	72	52	-	124
1958	72,584	31	43	1	75
1959	70,459		*record ends*		

works=heavy and light repairs at main works
shed=shed repairs and examinations
n/req= not required

Total Recorded Mileage 1,494,304
Withdrawn week ending 26/1/63
Cut up Crewe Works 6/63

Repairs LMS

13/4/39-28/4/39**LS**	8/8/44-2/9/44**HG**
18/1/40-8/2/40**LS**	19/5/45-9/6/45**LS**
6/11/40-5/1/41**HG**	2/1/46-16/3/46**HS**
3/1/42-7/2/42**LS**	28/4/47-20/5/47**HS**
30/3/42-18/4/42**LO**	18/10/47-10/11/47**NC**
12/11/42-5/12/42**HS**	15/1/48-14/2/48**LO**
31/7/43-20/8/43**LS**	6/9/48-26/10/48**HG**

46234 DUCHESS OF ABERCORN rattling the teacups in north London with the down 'Perth', which followed The Mid-Day Scot. The train is leaving Kensal Green tunnel on 20 June 1959, DUCHESS OF ABERCORN exuding all the vast thrilling strength which powered it to those feats of working in 1939, when it proved the efficacy of the double chimney and blastpipe. Photograph Peter Groom.

46234 DUCHESS OF ABERCORN

Built Crewe 4/8/38, cost £9,181 (engine), £1,478 (tender)
Built without streamlining
Renumbered 6234 to 46234 week ending 30/10/48

Repairs BR

[Dates in first column are from out of traffic to return to traffic; the two 'mileage' figures represent, firstly the miles accumulated since the previous General or Intermediate and secondly (the generally lower figure) the miles run up from January 1st of the year of shopping. All are recorded as taking place at Crewe unless otherwise noted. StR=St Rollox]

Dates	Weekdays Waiting	Weekdays On Works	Mileage	'Jan 1' Mileage
9/2/50-10/3/50**HI**	?	?	92,744	6,406
13/3/50-31/3/50**NC**		134	6,540	
8/4/50-2/5/50**NC**	?	604	7,011	
13/2/51-20/3/51**LI**	2	28	66,813	8,594
19/1/52-29/2/52**HG**	4	31	64,456	3,105
19/2/53-21/3/53**HI**	9	17	86,472	12,609
18/8/53-29/9/53**LC**	8	28	38,041	50,650
17/3/54-24/4/54**HG**	2	30	77,291	15,680
26/7/54-31/7/54**NC***	-	5	18,782	34,462
24/8/55-30/9/55**LI**	6	26	97,915	42,216
15/10/55-29/11/55**HC*** 11		27	1,540	43,756
15/5/57-5/7/57**HG**	4	40	124,613	26,823
13/8/57-14/9/57**HC***	8	20	7,813	34,636
19/3/58-25/4/58**LC***	4	27	45,761	17,691
25/1/59-28/2/59**LI**	1	28	105,934	5,280
25/2/60-13/4/60**HI**	12	29	73,201	7,722
7/6/60-18/8/60**LC***	33	29	15,729	23,451
28/8/61-25/10/61**HI**	16	34	87,428	37,922

record ends
*='(EO)' - 'Engine Only'

Sheds

Camden	13/8/38
Crewe (loan)	20/3/43
Edge Hill (loan)	20/5/44#
Crewe North	20/5/44#
Crewe North	19/8/44
Camden (loan)	18/10/47
Crewe North	15/11/47
Camden	20/6/59
Crewe North	7/11/59#
Camden	7/11/59#
Crewe North	21/11/59#
Carlisle Upperby	21/11/59#

#Nominal? dates the same
Stored we 1/12/62 to we 26/1/63

Tenders

No	Fitted
9752	4/8/38

Boilers

Fitted	No.	From
3/1/41	10297	6225
2/9/44	10294	6242
16/3/46	10300	6231
26/10/48	10305	6224
29/2/52	10293	-
24/4/54	9941	-
5/7/57	12470	-

No record after this date

Repairs LMS

28/3/40-22/4/40**TRO**	7/3/46-24/4/46**LS**
22/8/40-11/9/40**LS**	6/12/46-25/1/47**HG**
16/6/41-8/7/41**LS**	18/5/47-5/7/47**LO**
16/4/42-5/5/42**LS**	15/11/47-20/11/47**NC**
25/5/43-22/6/43**HG**	15/4/48-25/5/48**HS**
26/10/43-12/11/43**LO**	28/8/48-9/9/48**LO**
3/1/44-1/2/44**LO**	1/10/48-5/10/48**NC**
14/4/44-17/5/44**LS**	7/3/49-12/4/49**LO**
17/10/44-25/11/44**HS**	21/9/49-15/10/49**LI**
18/7/45-2/8/45**LO**	1/1/50-14/1/50**NC**
4/11/45-6/12/45**LO**	10/10/50-2/12/50**HG**

46235 CITY OF BIRMINGHAM

Built Crewe 27/6/39, cost £9,290 (engine), £1,548 (tender)
Built streamlined, casing removed 24/4/46
Renumbered 6235 to 46235 week ending 29/5/48

46235 CITY OF BIRMINGHAM at Crewe 20 October 1955. It was later to find a home in the Birmingham Museum, though it nearly never made it, being lucky to escape so lightly a collision high on a viaduct in May 1947.

LMS 'Summary' (this became 'Annual Statistics' from 1951)

Year	Mileage	Weekdays out of service			
		wks	shed	n/req	total
1939	36,308	-	25	-	37#
1940	69,578	40	70	2	112
1941	85,915	20	56	-	76
1942	77,937	17	68	-	85
1943	77,416	41	44	-	85
1944	54,968	94	42	1	137
1945	54,439	42	58	-	100
1946	57,431	60	43	-	103
1947	49,693	66	48	3	117
1948	53,594	46	66	2	114
1949	63,678	54	26	8	88
1950	54,105	55	58	6	119
1951	73,157	34	52	-	86
1952	75,711	27	56	-	83
1953	55,590	90	57	-	147
1954	76,522	-	72	1	73
1955	67,879	35	40	14	89
1956	72,275	40	34	1	75
1957	76,341	-	51	-	51
1958	72,504	-	51	-	51
1959	79,832	37	55	-	92
1060	52,752		*record ends*		
1961	56,268				
1962	45,159				
1963	27,625				

#'includes 12 days stored serviceable'
wks=heavy and light repairs at main works
shed=shed repairs and examinations
n/req= not required

Total Recorded Mileage 1,566,677
Withdrawn week ending 12/9/64
Preserved at Birmingham Museum

Repairs BR

[Dates in first column are from out of traffic to return to traffic; the two 'mileage' figures represent, firstly the miles accumulated since the previous General or Intermediate and secondly (the generally lower figure) the miles run up from January 1st of the year of shopping. All are recorded as taking place at Crewe unless otherwise noted. StR=St Rollox]

Dates	Weekdays Waiting	Weekdays On Works	Mileage	'Jan 1' Mileage
11/12/50-21/12/50**NC**	-	9	121	53,732
21/9/51-31/10/51**HI**	9	25	62,089	61,595
21/4/52-22/5/52**LC***	7	20	39,178	27,616
29/1/53-15/5/53**HG**	6	84	94,098	6,825
25/2/55-7/4/55**HG**	4	31	136,666	11,379
12/8/56-28/9/56**LI**	3	37	108,780	52,280
28/11/56-1/12/56**NC***	-	3	12,069	64,349
6/3/57-9/3/57**NC***	-	3	31,640	11,645
25/8/57-28/8/57**NC***	-	2	68,392	48,397
14/1/58-26/2/58**HG**	2	35	98,359	2,023
20/5/59-27/6/59**HI**	5	28	103,028	32,547
1/11/60-17/1/61**HG**	23	41	100,037	52,752

record ends
*='(EO)' - 'Engine Only'

Sheds

Crewe (loan)	1/7/39
Longsight	16/9/39
Rugby	30/9/39
Camden	21/10/39
Crewe North	20/5/44

Stored 14/9/39-21/9/39, 27/9/39-2/10/39, 6/11/62-3/1/63, 1/10/63-12/12/63

Tenders

No	Fitted
9798	27/6/39

Boilers

Fitted	No.	From
22/6/43	10299	6230
25/1/47	9939	6220
25/5/48	10641	6230
2/12/50	10299	6227
15/5/53	10693	-
7/4/55	10291	-
26/2/58	10646	-
17/1/61	9940	-

No record after this date

46236 CITY OF BRADFORD

Built Crewe 27/7/39, cost £9,290 (engine), £1,548 (tender)
Built streamlined, casing removed 10/7/48
Renumbered 6236 to 46236 week ending 17/7/48

46236 CITY OF BRADFORD was the LM's Pacific for the 1948 Locomotive Exchanges. Here it is during the trials, in April/May 1948, in its scintillating LMS black livery, about to leave Wakefield with the 1pm to Kings Cross.

Boilers

Fitted	No.	From
11/10/41	10643	new
19/7/45	10289	6224
27/2/48	10643	6231
30/11/51	12470	-
24/11/54	10306	-
11/7/58	10637	-
17/2/62	10301	-

No record after this date

Repairs BR

[Dates in first column are from out of traffic to return to traffic; the two 'mileage' figures represent, firstly the miles accumulated since the previous General or Intermediate and secondly (the generally lower figure) the miles run up from January 1st of the year of shopping. All are recorded as taking place at Crewe unless otherwise noted. StR=St Rollox]

Dates	Weekdays Waiting	Weekdays On Works	Mileage	'Jan 1' Mileage
11/1/51-10/2/51LC	7	19	34,958	2,523
19/10/51-30/11/51HG	9	27	89,513	57,078
10/6/52-5/8/52HI	5	43	52,641	46,228
23/9/53-24/10/53LI	5	22	98,135	60,561
18/10/54-24/11/54HG	2	30	89,773	71,845
12/4/55-21/5/55LC*	12	22	35,153	28,369
12/3/56-19/4/56HI	6	26	107,763	15,599
10/5/57-15/6/57LI	2	29	102,505	32,705
26/7/57-27/7/57NC*	-	1	8,895	41,600
26/5/58-11/7/58HG	1	39	83,771	29,945
17/3/59-25/3/59NC*	1(Rugby)	6	50,758	16,105
28/8/59-5/11/59LI	16	43	86,894	52,241
24/12/59-18/1/60LC	7	12	13,710	301
19/7/60-3/9/60LC*	14	26	51,226	37,817
23/9/60-18/10/60NC	15	6	-	-

record ends
=(EO)' - 'Engine Only'

Sheds

Camden	29/7/39
Longsight	16/9/39
Rugby	30/9/39
Camden	21/10/39
Edge Hill (loan)	20/5/44
Crewe North	8/7/44
Carlisle Upperby (loan)	19/7/47
Crewe North	18/10/47
Camden	24/4/48
Crewe North	10/7/48
Camden (loan)	23/6/51
Camden	7/7/51
Carlisle Upperby	14/6/58
Carlisle Kingmoor	3/11/62

Stored 12/9/39-21/9/39, 23/9/39-2/10/39, 30/12/63-27/1/64

Tenders

No	Fitted
9799	27/7/39
A79294	10/6/48#
9799	21/6/48
9749	21/1/49
9807	24/12/52

'Ex-Western Region'

LMS 'Summary' (this became 'Annual Statistics' from 1951)

Year	Mileage	Weekdays out of service			
		wks	shed	n/req	total
1939	28,129	-	19	18	54*
1940	83,699	16	65	5	86
1941	68,033	51	66	-	117
1942	73,216	28	64	-	92
1943	76,572	54	41	-	95
1944	65,126	49	85	1	135
1945	57,725	43	74	1	118
1946	63,587	22	73	-	95
1947	50,976	55	73	-	128
1948	59,617	53	57	1	111
1949	62,416	48	44	10	102
1950	60,902	35	22	17	74
1951	63,491	62	40	-	102
1952	83,802	48	44	-	92
1953	78,489	27	63	-	90
1954	78,629	32	66	-	98
1955	85,380	34	50	12	96
1956	85.399	32	54	-	86
1957	86,531	31	50	-	81
1958	64,598	40	78	1	119
1959	65,650		*record ends*		
1960	57,819				
1961	40,059				
1962	57,082				
1963	25,885				

wks=heavy and light repairs at main works
shed=shed repairs and examinations
n/req= not required
(stored 17 days)

Total Recorded Mileage 1,629,412
Withdrawn week ending 14/3/64
Cut up Crewe Works 4/64

Repairs LMS

8/7/40-25/7/40LS
24/4/41-10/5/41LS
15/9/41-11/10/41HG
13/12/41-10/1/42LO
15/1/42-2/2/42LO
5/3/43-29/3/43HS
16/9/43-23/10/43LO
23/3/44-15/4/44HS
3/11/44-9/12/44LO
31/5/45-19/7/45HG
20/8/46-13/9/46LS
29/4/47-2/6/47HO
28/11/47-27/2/48HG
15/4/48-16/4/48NC
7/6/48-10/6/48#
26/6/48-2/7/48NC
17/2/49-21/2/49No Repair
3/6/49-28/7/49HI
23/3/50-6/4/50LC
6/6/50-3/7/50HI
#'nil'

You'll Remember those Black and White Days...

46237 CITY OF BRISTOL

Built Crewe 9/8/39, cost £9,290 (engine), £1,548 (tender)
Built streamlined, casing removed 7/3/47
Renumbered 6237 to 46237 week ending 3/7/48

46237 CITY OF BRISTOL at speed, approaching Rugby with the up Royal Scot on 29 April 1958. All Pacifics slipped at times, both starting and at speed, though whether the Coronations were better or worse than say, Bulleid or Peppercorn Pacifics, is a subject now so far distant from regular first-hand experience that it would be pointless to pursue it here. The degree of slipping seemed to vary in time and place and certainly intermittent correspondence in *The Railway Magazine* for instance, from the 1940s to the 1960s, drew attention to the Coronations and various slipping episodes. Apparently one slipped at Lime Street for an *hour* once but this is presumably exceptional! They also slipped at speed, but this was all rather in the nature of the beast and a Pacific that didn't slip was a 4-6-0... Photograph Michael Mensing.

LMS 'Summary' (this became 'Annual Statistics' from 1951)

Year	Mileage	Weekdays out of service			
		wks	shed	n/req	total
1939	22,087	15	8	16	56*
1940	92,195	26	58	2	86
1941	79,111	31	68	1	100
1942	45,369	40	102	-	142
1943	76,514	51	45	-	96
1944	65,330	25	80	-	105
1945	75,162	51	44	1	96
1946	75,217	13	69	1	83
1947	56,052	85	53	-	138
1948	68,630	23	68	-	91
1949	71,801	37	47	1	85
1950	73,117	28	65	-	93
1951	69,173	62	46	-	108
1952	78,995	36	56	-	92
1953	78,821	50	44	-	94
1954	91,734	2	75	-	77
1955	74,070#	44	40	11	95
1956	60,565	77	48	-	125
1957	75,939	35	49	-	84
1958	80,498	31	51	3	85
1959	67,445		record ends		

#'includes miles run whilst on Western Region'
wks=heavy and light repairs at main works
shed=shed repairs and examinations
n/req= not required
*(includes 17 days 'stored serviceable')

Total Recorded Mileage 1,477,825
Withdrawn week ending 12/9/64
Cut up West of Scotland
Shipbreaking Co, Troon 12/64

Boilers

Fitted	No.	From
17/9/43	10293	6241
7/3/47	9938	6238
9/9/49	10290	6248
20/9/52	9940	-
16/3/55	10643	-
19/10/57	10639	-
18/2/59	10645	-
No record after this date		

Repairs BR

[Dates in first column are from out of traffic to return to traffic; the two 'mileage' figures represent, firstly the miles accumulated since the previous General or Intermediate and secondly (the generally lower figure) the miles run up from January 1st of the year of shopping. All are recorded as taking place at Crewe unless otherwise noted. StR=St Rollox]

Dates	Weekdays Waiting	Weekdays On Works	Mileage	'Jan 1' Mileage
21/7/50-23/8/50HI	5	23	63,310	36,106
27/4/51-1/6/51LI	8	22	63,755	26,744
26/10/51-3/12/51HC	12	20	36,601	63,345
9/8/52-20/9/52HG	8	28	96,768	54,339
16/2/53-19/3/53HC*	7	20	34,059	9,403
5/12/53-6/1/54LI	1	24	103,477	78,821
24/1/55-16/3/55HG	6	38	97,259	5,525
9/4/56-10/5/56LI	6	21	89,539	20,994
25/5/56-16/6/56LC*	9	10	1,973	22,967
4/7/56-9/8/56LC*	8	23	2,682	23,676
9/9/57-19/10/57HG	3	32	97,696	58,125
5/11/58-11/12/58LI	4	27	95,748	77,934
16/1/59-18/2/59HC*	-	28	3,151	687
19/7/60-10/9/60LI	8	38	110,544	40,535
21/8/61-14/10/61LI	15	32	54,095	34,072
24/10/61-31/10/61NC*	-	6	604	34,676

record ends
*='(EO)'- Engine Only

Sheds

Camden	12/8/39
Longsight	16/9/39
Rugby	30/9/39
Camden	21/10/39
Carlisle Upperby (loan)	10/5/52
Camden	24/5/52
Western Region	23/4/55
Camden	21/5/55
Carlisle Upperby	14/6/58
Carlisle Kingmoor	#
Carlisle Upperby	7/4/62
Carlisle Kingmoor	3/61

 # entry merely has '?'
stored 12/9/39-21/9/39, 23/9/39-2/10/39,
29/10/62-we2/2/63, 7/1/64-9/3/64

Tenders

No	Fitted
9800	9/8/39
9804	17/4/44
9800	6/5/44

Repairs LMS

1/11/39-17/11/39**LO**
28/8/40-21/9/40**LS**
24/12/40-15/1/41**LO**
16/6/41-3/7/41**LS**
14/3/42-4/4/42**LS**
1/12/42-24/12/42**LO**
6/3/43-23/3/43**LO**
7/8/43-17/9/43**HG**
26/7/44-23/8/44**HS**
20/4/45-10/5/45**LO**
23/10/45-30/11/45**HS**
23/11/46-7/12/46**TRO**
12/1/47-7/3/47**HG**
19/8/47-23/9/47**LO**
8/6/48-3/7/48**LS**
19/7/48-23/7/48**NC**
29/7/49-9/9/49**HG**

46237 CITY OF BRISTOL in blue, preparing to depart from Euston with the Royal Train about 1950. Photograph Alec Swain/ B.P. Hoper Collection.

On 19 April 1955 46237 CITY OF BRISTOL was transferred to the Western Region for a four week period of trials. The idea was to see what, if anything, could be done to improve the inconsistencies in the performance of the Kings, through comparison with other 8P types. The Western Region does not seem to have fallen over itself to express gratitude at this, and relations do not seem to have been wholly amicable. *The Railway Observer* records that the LM Inspector was fairly disgusted at CITY OF BRISTOL being put on the nine coach Merchant Venturer to Bristol. Announcing, sniffily, that it had brought seventeen coaches up from Carlisle to Euston the week before would not, probably, have endeared him to his WR compatriots... 46237 arrived three minutes late in Bristol, the first time such an LM Pacific had appeared in the city, and was tried on both the turntables at Bath Road shed. They were too short, and 46237 had to turn using the triangle out at North Somerset Junction. After this the 'big 'un' was to be set on the Cornish Riviera as well as the 9.10am Paddington - Birkenhead as far as Wolverhampton, returning with the 11.45 ex-Birkenhead, and it is presumably on this train, or one like it, when photographed at Snow Hill on 26 April 1955. Photograph F.W. Shuttleworth.

<table>
<tr><td colspan="2">**Repairs LMS**</td><td>3/1/45-3/2/45**HG**</td></tr>
<tr><td>9/8/40-31/8/40**LS**</td><td colspan="2">15/9/45-26/10/45**LS**</td></tr>
<tr><td>23/6/41-24/7/41**HG**</td><td colspan="2">8/11/46-10/1/47**HG**</td></tr>
<tr><td>3/6/42-27/6/42**LS**</td><td colspan="2">15/11/47-17/12/47**LS**</td></tr>
<tr><td>24/5/43-11/6/43**LS**</td><td colspan="2">3/1/49-4/3/49**HG**</td></tr>
<tr><td>23/5/44-19/6/44**HS**</td><td colspan="2">6/10/49-4/11/49**NC**</td></tr>
</table>

46238 CITY OF CARLISLE

Built Crewe 14/9/39, cost £9,290 (engine), £1,548 (tender)
Built streamlined, casing removed 10/1/47
Renumbered 6238 to 46238 week ending 5/3/49

Ye Grate Beeste in its lair. 46238 CITY OF CARLISLE, far too splendid to let that ghastly stripe detract from its immense dignity, inside Upperby roundhouse in the 1960s. The 'speedo' of 1957 is prominent on the rear driving wheel. The hollow axles, machined so to reduce weight, are also shown to good effect. Photograph J.G. Walmsley, B.P. Hoper Collection.

LMS 'Summary' (this became 'Annual Statistics' from 1951)

Year	Mileage	Weekdays out of service			
		wks	shed	n/req	total
1939	18,327	-	13	20	38#
1940	86.876	20	51	11	82
1941	82.697	28	45	-	73
1942	77,629	22	66	1	89
1943	78,195	17	58	-	75
1944	74,788	24	49	2	75
1945	76,122	64	34	2	100
1946	67,740	43	65	3	111
1947	65,434	39	64	2	105
1948	70,734	-	74	-	74
1949	56,983	53	66	3	122
1950	67,005	21	67	5	93
1951	64,920	45	56	2	103
1952	60,779	48	50	6	104
1953	61,642	32	75	9	116
1954	60,203	-	95	9	104
1955	55,382	41	63	10	114
1956	75,537	-	82	7	89
1957	74,516	23	59	10	92
1958	60,039	39	78	7	124
1959	65,356		*record ends*		
1960	79,617				
1961	42,490				
1962	38,832				
1963	39,776				

#'stored serviceable five days'
wks=heavy and light repairs at main works
shed=shed repairs and examinations
n/req= not required

Total Recorded Mileage 1,602,628
Withdrawn week ending 12/9/64
Cut up West of Scotland
Shipbreaking Co, Troon 12/64

Repairs BR

[Dates in first column are from out of traffic to return to traffic; the two 'mileage' figures represent, firstly the miles accumulated since the previous General or Intermediate and secondly (the generally lower figure) the miles run up from January 1st of the year of shopping. All are recorded as taking place at Crewe unless otherwise noted. StR=St Rollox]

Dates	Weekdays Waiting	Weekdays On Works	Mileage	'Jan 1' Mileage
8/5/50-1/6/50**LI**	-	20	74,551	17,725
4/4/51-15/5/51**LI**	9	26	67,884	18,604
18/5/51-30/5/51**NC**	-	10	Nil	18,604
22/2/52-29/3/52**HG**	2	29	56,612	10,296
19/4/52-9/5/52**NC**	6	11	4,207	14,503
14/8/53-21/9/53**HI**	2	32	90,516	40,033
10/8/55-27/9/55**HG**	4	37	116,607	34,795
27/3/56-5/4/56**NC***	-	7	35,768	15,181
4/1/57-31/1/57**LI**	3	20	96,296	172
16/11/57-21/11/57**NC***	1	3	67,509	67,681
6/5/58-20/6/58**HI**	12	27	100,897	26,553
12/12/59-12/2/60**HI**	13	38	98,842	65,356
29/5/61-4/7/61**HG**	1	30	98,197	18,580
31/7/61-15/9/61**LC***	15	25	3,821	22,401

record ends
*=(EO)- Engine Only

Sheds

Crewe	16/9/39
Camden	21/10/39
Carlisle Upperby	24/5/47
Camden	10/6/50
Carlisle Upperby	30/9/50
Camden	7/7/51
Carlisle Upperby	15/9/51
Camden	10/5/52
Carlisle Upperby	24/5/52

Stored 24/9/39-2/10/39, 2/1/64-27/1/64

Tenders
No	Fitted
9801	14/9/39

Boilers

Fitted	No.	From
24/7/44	10641	new
3/2/45	9938	6223
10/1/47	10637	6221
4/3/49	10302	6226
29/3/52	10298	-
27/9/55	10693	-
4/7/61	10287	-

No record after this date

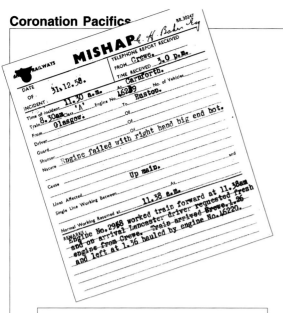

MISHAP

RAILWAYS

TELEPHONE REPORT RECEIVED
FROM Crewe.
TIME RECEIVED 3.0 p.m.

DATE 31.12.58.
OF
INCIDENT 11.30 a.m. At Carnforth.
Time of incident 'A' Engine No. 46239 Euston.
Train 8.30am Class No. of Vehicles
From Glasgow. Of
Driver Of
Guard Of
Shunter Of
Nature Engine failed with right hand big end hot.
and
Cause Up main. At
Lines Affected
Single Line Working Between 11.38 a.m.
Normal Working Resumed at 11.38 a.m.
REMARKS: No.2968 worked train forward at 11.38am
and on arrival Lancaster driver requested fresh
engine from Crewe. Train arrived Crewe 1.26
and left at 1.36 hauled by engine No.46220.

46239 CITY OF CHESTER

Built Crewe 29/8/39, cost £9,290 (engine), £1,548 (tender)
Built streamlined, casing removed 23/9/47
Renumbered 6239 to 46239 week ending 21/8/48

Repairs BR

[Dates in first column are from out of traffic to return to traffic; the two 'mileage' figures represent, firstly the miles accumulated since the previous General or Intermediate and secondly (the generally lower figure) the miles run up from January 1st of the year of shopping. All are recorded as taking place at Crewe unless otherwise noted. StR=St Rollox]

Dates	Weekdays	Weekdays Waiting	Mileage On Works	'Jan 1' Mileage
28/4/52-30/5/52**HG**	3	25	76,507	32,240
24/3/53-6/5/53**HI**	11	26	79,369	22,008
25/9/53-23/10/53**LC***	3	21	43,097	65,105
13/7/54-27/8/54**HG**	5	34	108,330	46,819
24/10/55-29/11/55**LI**	12	19	97,030	68,293
8/2/57-15/3/57**HG**	3	27	110,812	10,897
26/3/57-5/4/57**NC***	-	9	-	-
6/8/57-21/8/57**NC***	11	2	34,070	44,967
21/1/58-1/3/58**HI**	4	30	75,008	5,034
2/2/59-13/3/59**HG**	1	33	87,224	9,565
5/7/60-19/8/60**HI**	14	25	118,066	45,099
30/10/60-15/12/60**LC***	16	20	17,987	63,086
1/7/61-28/8/61**LC***	22	27	57,201	35,598

record ends
='(EO)'- Engine Only*

Sheds

Camden	2/9/39
Crewe	16/9/39
Camden	21/10/39
Polmadie (loan)	2/12/39
Camden	3/2/40
Holyhead (loan)	6/4/40
Camden	1/6/40
Polmadie (loan)	14/10/44
Camden	11/11/44
Holyhead	24/8/63

Stored 10/9/39-2/10/39,
11/11/62-8/12/62,
22/9/63-1/12/63

Tenders

No	Fitted
9802	29/8/39
9747	22/11/45

Repairs LMS

16/9/40-5/10/40**LO**
13/2/41-7/3/41**LO**
9/9/41-29/9/41**LS**
14/9/42-3/10/42**LS**
8/6/43-3/7/43**HS**
25/3/44-22/4/44**HG**
24/4/45-1/6/45**LS**
3/4/46-6/5/46**LS**
12/5/47-23/9/47**HG**
12/7/48-19/8/48**LS**
12/1/49-8/2/49**NC**
29/7/49-2/9/49**LI**
14/9/49-21/9/49**NC**
23/9/49-10/10/49**NC**
20/2/50-3/3/50**NC**
8/6/50-3/7/50**HG**
7/7/50-4/8/50**NC#**
26/5/51-23/6/51**LI**
#*'owing to incidence of Works Holidays Engine was sent into traffic unpainted. Returned to Shops for painting 14/7/50'*

Boilers

Fitted	No.	From
22/4/44	9941	6226
23/9/47	10693	6251
3/7/50	10297	6223
30/5/52	10300	-
27/8/54	10640	-
15/3/57	10294	-
13/3/59	10306	-

No record after this date

LMS 'Summary' (this became 'Annual Statistics' from 1951)

Year	Mileage	Weekdays out of service			
		works	shed	n/req	total
1939	20,000	-	9	18	46#
1940	79,604	18	77	15	110
1941	84,342	38	40	-	78
1942	77,443	18	55	-	73
1943	88,657	23	38	-	61
1944	66,800	25	89	-	114
1945	62,961	33	91	1	125
1946	67,479	19	103	5	127
1947	47,285	115	51	-	166
1948	74,064	34	43	1	78
1949	64,196	53	58	1	112
1950	72,601	45	50	-	95
1951	78,782	24	62	-	86
1952	89,601	28	54	-	82
1953	80,519	61	40	-	101
1954	75,556	39	64	-	103
1955	74,094	31	87	7	125
1956	94,114	-	78	-	78
1957	80,871	39	58	-	97
1958	82,693	34	78	1	112
1959	82,532		*record ends*		

#*'includes19 days stored serviceable*
works=heavy and light repairs at main works
shed=shed repairs and examinations
n/req= not required

Total Recorded Mileage 1,544,194
Withdrawn week ending 12/9/64
Cut up J.Cashmore, Great Bridge 12/64

46239 CITY OF CHESTER, by now a Willesden engine (though its Record Card will not admit it) waits, shrouded in steam, to move off the shed. Indeed Willesden, a vast, half-ruined smoky vault of a place in north London built principally for freight workings, provided an unlikely showcase for some of the last work of the Coronations. *The Railway Observer* noted that on 5 July 1964 no less than seven Coronations were on shed there: *'probably the maximum present here at any one time, being 46225(12B), 46238(12B), 46239(1A), 46240(1A), 46241(8A), 46245(1A) and 46248(5A), with 46240 and 46245 in their accustomed immaculate condition'.* Indeed, the great days of Camden seem to have been briefly recreated. As well as the Stanier Pacifics two Royal Scots had turned up that day and there were *eight* Jubilees and another eight Britannias. Photograph J.G. Walmsley, B.P. Hoper Collection.

46240 CITY OF COVENTRY

Built Crewe 27/3/40, cost £9,290 (engine), £1,548 (tender)
Built streamlined, casing removed 29/7/47
Renumbered 6240 to 46240 week ending 26/6/48

The Railway Observer was certainly correct when it referred to the immaculate condition of 46240 CITY OF COVENTRY. Pictures of it at Willesden shed illustrate something of the undiminished grandeur of the dear old thing, in glorious red in the 1960s, even as its end drew near. The condition of the Britannia Pacific in the background is ample testimony to the fact that a special effort was being made for 46240. Photograph J.G. Walmsley, B.P. Hoper Collection.

LMS 'Summary' *(this became 'Annual Statistics' from 1951)*

Year	Mileage	Weekdays out of service			
		works	shed	n/req	total
1940	71,148	-	54	1	55
1941	83,612	20	57	-	77
1942	75,720	28	55	1	84
1943	59,965	69	52	-	121
1944	72,457	42	66	-	108
1945	52,898	67	64	6	137
1946	74,620	28	71	1	100
1947	56,181	72	74	-	146
1948	58,646	55	64	2	121
1949	72,338	25	67	2	94
1950	88,950	16	58	-	74
1951	67,538	82	28	1	111
1952	80,320	26	64	1	91
1953	78,544	49	60	-	109
1954	77,481	38	59	2	99
1955	92,974	6	53	12	71
1956	77,462	52	55	-	107
1957	74,944	39	66	-	105
1958	80,612	38	65	-	103
1959	95,633			*record ends*	
1960	67,850				
1961	58,002				
1962	30,647				
1963	28,480				

works=heavy and light repairs at main works
shed=shed repairs and examinations
n/req= not required

Total Recorded Mileage 1,685,042
Withdrawn week ending 12/9/64
Cut up J.Cashmore, Great Bridge 3/65

Repairs BR

[Dates in first column are from out of traffic to return to traffic; the two 'mileage' figures represent, firstly the miles accumulated since the previous General or Intermediate and secondly (the generally lower figure) the miles run up from January 1st of the year of shopping. All are recorded as taking place at Crewe unless otherwise noted. StR=St Rollox]

Dates	Weekdays Waiting	Weekdays On Works	Mileage	'Jan 1' Mileage
23/12/50-2/2/51**LI**	8	26	89,109	159
17/6/51-21/7/51**LC**	-	29	32,614	32,773
26/9/51-25/10/51**LC***	9	16	50,109	50,268
3/6/52-3/7/52**HG**	1	25	105,676	38,297
3/6/53-30/7/53**LI**	11	38	83,057	41,034
22/9/54-29/10/54**HG**	-	32	102,867	65,357
10/12/54-17/12/54**LC***	-	6	8,180	73,537
23/12/55-28/1/56**HI**	2	27	105,098	92,974
29/5/56-2/7/56**LC***	-	29	33,440	33,440
25/3/57-10/5/57**LI**	7	32	92,777	15,315
16/8/57-16/8/57**NC***	-	1	24,489	39,804
3/6/58-17/7/58**HG**	2	36	94,787	35,158
21/4/59-30/5/59**HI**	12	22	76,274	39,820
6/6/60-20/8/60**HI**	19	46	98,158	33,348

record ends
*= '(EO)'- Engine Only

Sheds

Crewe	30/3/40
Camden	13/4/40
Willesden	7/9/63
Stored 18/11/62-8/12/62,	
22/9/63-1/12/63	

Tenders

No	Fitted
9803	27/3/40
9703	29/6/44
9803	6/8/44

Repairs LMS

19/2/41-11/3/41**LS**	20/8/45-28/9/45**LO**
11/3/42-2/4/42**LS**	7/1/46-7/2/46**HS**
16/4/42-24/4/42**LO**	8/5/47-30/7/47**HG**
21/1/43-15/2/43**LS**	22/10/47-30/10/47**NC**
9/10/43-6/11/43**HG**	28/5/48-25/6/48**LS**
30/11/43-4/1/44**LO**	15/9/48-21/10/48**HO**
16/11/44-22/12/44**LS**	7/9/49-19/9/49**NC**
29/12/44-6/2/45**LO**	2/12/49-13/1/50**HG**

Boilers

Fitted	No.	From
6/11/43	10306	6229
30/7/47	10291	6225
13/1/50	10304	6243
3/7/52	9938	-
29/10/54	10289	-
17/7/58	9939	-
13/4/62	9941	-

From the cab window of 46240 at Willesden. That vast bulk of boiler must have started to put sweat on the brow of any Fireman, before a single shovelfull was swung... Photograph J.G. Walmsley, B.P. Hoper Collection.

Far to the north, 46240 CITY OF COVENTRY at Perth on 21 July 1964, waiting to leave (such was their lot by now) with the 2.11pm Aberdeen - Manchester fish train. The spotters had done well that day, for the train had come in earlier behind A4 60023 GOLDEN EAGLE. Seldom could fish have enjoyed a more illustrious passage. Photograph Malcolm Castledine.

A gleaming CITY OF COVENTRY ready to go at Willesden. Photograph J.G. Walmsley, B.P. Hoper Collection.

LMS 'Summary' (this became 'Annual Statistics' from 1951)

Year	Mileage	Weekdays out of service			
		works	shed	n/req	total
1940	61,318	-	54	2	56
1941	79,381	33	52	1	86
1942	74,249	24	47	-	71
1943	69,934	25	56	-	81
1944	42,182	32	85	-	117
1945	72,519	69	58	-	127
1946	73,588	16	80	4	100
1947	68,349	34	56	3	93
1948	71,395	34	54	3	91
1949	73,154	50	57	1	108
1950	79,569	38	42	-	80
1951	64,080	41	63	-	104
1952	76,433	20	85	1	106
1953	54,625	134	57	-	191
1954	81,865	45	37	-	82
1955	69,181	22	74	14	110
1956	75,775	38	77	-	115
1957	84,615	-	73	-	73
1958	80,255	35	59	-	94
1959	73,520		record ends		

works=heavy and light repairs at main works
shed=shed repairs and examinations
n/req= not required

Total Recorded Mileage 1,425,987
Withdrawn week ending 5/9/64
Cut up J.Cashmore, Great Bridge 1/65

Repairs LMS

28/3/41-17/4/41**LS**
10/12/41-9/1/42**LS**
14/3/42-28/3/42**LO**
1/5/43-29/5/43**HG**
8/9/44-14/10/44**HS**
7/5/45-16/6/45**LO**
31/10/45-8/12/45**LS**
10/12/46-6/2/47**HG**
12/1/48-21/1/48**NC**
17/4/48-26/5/48**HS**
4/8/49-30/9/49**HG**
21/10/49-31/10/49**NC**

Boilers

Fitted	No.	From
29/5/43	10640	6232
6/2/47	10694	6252
30/9/49	10295	6252
11/6/53	10294	-
3/11/56	10637	-
11/2/58	10643	-

No record after this date

46241 CITY OF EDINBURGH

Built Crewe 3/4/40, cost £9,290 (engine), £1,548 (tender)
Built streamlined, casing removed 6/2/47
Renumbered 6241 to 46241 week ending 29/5/48

Repairs BR

[Dates in first column are from out of traffic to return to traffic; the two 'mileage' figures represent, firstly the miles accumulated since the previous General or Intermediate and secondly (the generally lower figure) the miles run up from January 1st of the year of shopping. All are recorded as taking place at Crewe unless otherwise noted. StR=St Rollox]

Dates	Weekdays Waiting	Weekdays On Works	Mileage	'Jan 1' Mileage
13/9/50-10/10/50**LI**	-	23	87,252	66,434
17/10/50-3/11/50**NC**	-	15	394	66,828
17/6/51-3/7/51**HC**	-	13	48,232	35,097
16/10/51-17/11/51**HI**	2	26	67,762	54,627
18/2/52-14/3/52**NC**	6	16	21,939	12,486
8/5/52-31/5/52**LC***	6	14	35,005	25,552
3/3/53-11/6/53**HG**	1	84	98,938	13,052
12/7/53-16/8/53**LC***	-	30('shed')	7,242	'to follow'
12/9/53-5/10/53**LC***	9	10	15,724	28,776
4/5/54-28/5/54**HI**	1	20	75,283	33,710
15/11/54-13/12/54**LC***	6	18	44,548	78,258
27/9/55-22/10/55**HI**	-	22	108,547	60,392
20/9/56-3/11/56**HG**	12	26	72,692	63,903
21/11/57-25/11/57**NC***	-	3	89,306	77,434
1/1/58-11/2/58**HG**	4	31	96,568	81
27/1/59-7/3/59**HI**	6	28	88,020	6,241
6/2/60-20/5/60**HI#**	26	62	74,491	8,817
31/7/61-21/9/61**HI#**	3	42		78,165
30,435				

#'boiler lifted out and put back'
record ends
*='(EO)'- Engine Only

Sheds

Crewe	6/4/40
Camden	13/4/40
Edge Hill	26/10/57
Camden	16/11/57
Crewe North	20/9/58

Stored 5/11/62-we 2/2/63, 14/10/63-23/3/64

Tenders

No	Fitted
9804	3/4/40
9805	13/3/44
9811	1/8/53
9703	21/9/56
9811	3/11/56

A Camden 'Semi', 46241 CITY OF EDINBURGH, with another behind, standing outside the shed. A severely bent and crumpled 'Not to be Moved' board projects gamely from the cab. Camden was first converted for diesel servicing by partitioning off some of the roads (about 1957) and then, when Type 4s had ousted all the Pacifics and 4-6-0s, was more or less demolished, leaving the diesels standing in the open. Photograph Alec Swain/B.P. Hoper Collection.

LMS 'Summary' (this became 'Annual Statistics' from 1951)

Year	Mileage	wks	shed	n/req	total
1940	55,083	-	42	-	42
1941	82,687	22	55	-	77
1942	77,296	44	31	-	75
1943	84,947	21	53	-	74
1944	74,685	22	46	4	72
1945	62,791	29	93	1	123
1946	71,536	18	82	-	100
1947	53,954	51	76	-	127
1948	77,815	38	64	2	104
1949	64,539	60	54	2	116
1950	79,047	27	55	-	82
1951	63,713	38	88	2	128
1952	58,563	67	44	-	111
1953	13,953	257	4	-	261
1954	79,711	36	24	2	62
1955	76,401	24	73	15	112
1956	83,063	35	71	-	106
1957	81,195	22	73	-	95
1958	81,826	36	57		93
1959	76,772		record ends		
1960	76,595				
1961	46,585				
1962	32,523				

wks=heavy and light repairs at main works
shed=shed repairs and examinations
n/req= not required

Total Recorded Mileage 1,555,280
Withdrawn week ending 19/10/63
Cut up Crewe Works 11/63

Repairs LMS
28/4/41-22/5/41**LS**
27/2/42-21/3/42**LS**
21/9/42-17/10/42**LO**
2/6/43-29/6/43**LS**
12/5/44-6/6/44**HG**
19/3/45-20/4/45**HS**
16/5/46-5/6/46**LS**
6/3/47-3/5/47**HG**
5/11/47-10/11/47**NC**
14/4/48-27/5/48**LS**
22/12/48-25/12/48**NC**
27/5/49/27/7/49**HG**
3/8/49-6/8/49**NC**

Boilers
Fitted	No.	From
6/6/42	10296	6244
2/5/47	10640	6241
29/7/49	13043	new
26/10/53	10299	-
17/4/57	10641	-
19/6/59	10639	-

No record after this date

46242 CITY OF GLASGOW

Built Crewe 15/5/40, cost £9,290 (engine), £1,548 (tender)
Built streamlined, casing removed 3/5/47
Renumbered 6242 to 46242 week ending 29/5/48
'involved in Harrow mishap 8/10/52'

Repairs BR
[Dates in first column are from out of traffic to return to traffic; the two 'mileage' figures represent, firstly the miles accumulated since the previous General or Intermediate and secondly (the generally lower figure) the miles run up from January 1st of the year of shopping. All are recorded as taking place at Crewe unless otherwise noted. StR=St Rollox]

Dates	Weekdays Waiting	Weekdays On Works	Mileage	'Jan 1' Mileage
16/5/50-16/6/50**HI**	5	22	71,341	34,654
12/6/51-26/7/51**HI**	2	36	81,389	36,996
21/5/52-21/6/52**LI**	4	23	56,838	30,121
9/10/52-26/10/53**HG**	33	291#	28,442	58,563
30/8/54-11/10/54**LI**	4	32	74,567	60,614
16/8/55-13/9/55**HI**	1	23	72,852	53,755
29/1/56-8/2/56**NC***	2	5	32,948	10,302
1/5/56-9/6/56**LI**	2	32	53,031	30,385
23/10/56-24/10/56**LC**	-	1	38,514	68,899
22/3/57-17/4/57**HG**	4	18	73,697	21,019
10/8/57-14/8/57**NC***	2	1	29,716	50,735
18/1/58-1/3/58**HI**	7	29	66,652	6,477
2/4/59-19/6/59**HG**	4	63	99,598	24,249
27/7/60-16/9/60**LI**	5	39	101,343	48,820
16/8/61-16/8/61**NC**	-	1(StR)	-	-
25/1/62-12/5/62**HI**	13	79	74,567	507

record ends
*='(EO)'- Engine Only
#Aftermath of Harrow collision

Sheds
Camden	18/5/40
Polmadie (loan)	22/7/44
Polmadie	26/8/44
Crewe North (loan)	12/6/48
Camden (loan)	26/6/48
Camden	14/8/48
Crewe North	27/6/53
Camden	20/11/54
Polmadie (initially loan)	11/3/61

Tenders
No	Fitted
9805	15/5/40
9804	13/3/44
9800	17/4/44
9804	6/5/44
9703	9/1/46
9816	26/7/51

46242 CITY OF GLASGOW on a Perth to Euston train, passing Shap summit, 19 July 1957. This, of course, was the engine involved in the Harrow disaster, which saw the end of the former Turbomotive, 46202 PRINCESS ANNE. 46242 was put back in order (the Harrow smash is the only one noted on the Record Cards) in due course. It was a matter of some comment, when it finally emerged from Crewe, that the front end had been renewed in the traditional draping curve in front of the cylinders, after the fashion of the original non-streamlined engines. Photograph L. Elsey.

46243 CITY OF LANCASTER

Built Crewe 29/5/40, cost £9,290 (engine), £1,548 (tender)
Built streamlined, casing removed 16/7/49
Renumbered from 6243 to 46243 week ending 24/4/48

LMS 'Summary' (this became 'Annual Statistics' from 1951)					
Year	Mileage	Weekdays out of service			
		wks	shed	n/req	total
1940	51,628	-	38	3	41
1941	76,247	39	50	-	89
1942	75,270	24	59	-	83
1943	60,243	63	57	-	120
1944	76,115	35	40	1	76
1945	75,512	33	53	1	87
1946	56,204	21	84	2	113
1947	65,764	20	99	1	120
1948	64,263	30	51	1	82
1949	59,223	45	47	11	103
1950	77,648	22	33	8	63
1951	68,291	29	55	1	85
1952	56,723	96	40	1	137
1953	79,040	40	53	-	93
1954	75,226	53	21	-	74
1955	70,420	31	28	1	60
1956	71,685	36	43	2	81
1957	70,546	34	53	-	87
1958	69,750	33	46	-	79
1959	74,787		record ends		
1960	73,702				
1961	35,891				
1962	30,305				
1963	11,809				

wks=heavy and light repairs at main works
shed=shed repairs and examinations
n/req= not required

Total Recorded Mileage 1,526,292
Withdrawn week ending 12/9/64
Cut up Central Wagon Co, Ince 8/65

Repairs BR

[Dates in first column are from out of traffic to return to traffic; the two 'mileage' figures represent, firstly the miles accumulated since the previous General or Intermediate and secondly (the generally lower figure) the miles run up from January 1st of the year of shopping. All are recorded as taking place at Crewe unless otherwise noted. StR=St Rollox]

Dates	Weekdays Waiting	Weekdays On Works	Mileage	'Jan 1' Mileage
11/5/50-6/6/50**LC**	2	20	67,430	29,365
29/3/51-2/5/51**LI**	4	25	130,084	14,371
3/6/52-23/9/52**HG**	7	89	86,081	32,161
16/4/53-28/5/53**LC**	16	20	51,648	27,086
30/12/53-5/2/54**HG**	8	24	103,602	79,040
2/12/54-7/1/55**HI**	1	28	75,226	75,226
9/11/55-10/12/55**LC**	10	17	67,331	67,331
7/8/56-18/9/56**HI**	1	35	119,222	48,802
5/9/57-7/9/57**NC***	-	2	75,690	52,807
8/10/57-16/11/57**HG**	1	33	83,019	60,136
3/9/58-11/10/58**HI**	5	28	64,220	53,801
19/10/59-18/12/59**HG**	14	38	88,207	72,267
27/7/60-5/8/60**NC***	11	14	51,618	49,098
30/5/61-14/8/61**HG**	17	48	93,824	17,602

record ends
*** = '(EO)'- Engine Only**

Sheds

Camden	1/6/40
Edge Hill	5/6/48
Crewe North	11/12/48
Carlisle Upperby	14/6/58
Crewe North	20/9/58
Camden	11/6/60

Stored 5/11/62-we2/2/63, 14/10/63-23/12/63, 30/12/63 to 23/3/64

Tenders

No	Fitted
9806	29/5/40

Boilers

Fitted	No.	From
24/12/43	10292	6240
22/2/46	10304	6226
22/6/49	10637	-
23/9/52	10640	-
5/2/54	10287	-
16/11/57	10293	-
18/12/59	10288	-
14/8/61	10290	-

No record after this date

Repairs LMS

7/3/41-29/3/41**LS**	24/7/45-30/8/45**LO**
11/10/41-1/11/41**LS**	23/1/46-22/2/46**HG**
21/10/42-17/11/42**LS**	17/4/47-9/5/47**HS**
13/5/43-4/6/43**LO**	23/9/47-18/10/47**NC**
5/11/43-24/12/43**HG**	16/3/48-20/4/48**LS**
27/10/44-6/12/44**HS**	1/5/49-22/6/49**HG**

46243 CITY OF LANCASTER on the 10.00am Liverpool to Euston, at Rugby 1 September 1962. That such an engine and train could be more or less lost in a scene such as this is a measure of just *how much* railway there was then. Photograph B.P. Hoper Collection.

Glory and Trumpets! 46244 KING GEORGE VI at Carlisle Citadel in 1955. Photograph J. Robertson, B.P. Hoper Collection.

6244 KING GEORGE VI as red streamliner, newly renamed from CITY OF LEEDS in April 1941. This picture shows well the hollow axles and the motion, which played such a role in the drive for weight reduction. 'Vibrac' steel was used and fluted sections never gave any problems of note. There was none of the reversion to straight section rods often seen in the case of the BR Standards. The new steel was stronger and lighter than the manganese-molybdenum used in the Princess Pacifics; indeed, though at 11ft the connecting rods were 2ft longer than those on the Princesses, the new rods were 7lb lighter. This engine was involved in one of the worst accidents (five passengers died) which the Coronations experienced. In this streamlined form it entered Crewe for repair and emerged in September without the casing. It was derailed between Atherstone and Polesworth in July 1947.

LMS 'Summary' (this became 'Annual Statistics' from 1951)

Year	Mileage	Weekdays out of service			
		wks	shed	n/req	total
1940	33,184	-	33	1	34
1941	76,017	29	64	2	95
1942	71,195	29	40	-	69
1943	65,397	75	36	-	111
1944	77,829	12	87	-	99
1945	70,367	26	58	5	89
1946	81,053	25	63	7	95
1947	57,470	68	61	1	130
1948	64,363	69	41	2	112
1949	75,564	44	57	-	101
1950	59,736	65	52	-	117
1951	88,245	26	42	-	68
1952	73,565	63	44	-	107
1953	62,301	82	59	-	141
1954	77,935	31	62	-	93
1955	68,549	48	63	14	125
1956	79,879	32	68	-	100
1957	70,978	40	64	-	104
1958	67,900	35	72	5	112
1959	78,626			record ends	

wks=heavy and light repairs at main works
shed=shed repairs and examinations
n/req= not required

Total Recorded Mileage 1,400,154
Withdrawn week ending 12/9/64
Cut up West of Scotland
Shipbreaking Co, Troon 12/64

Repairs LMS

3/5/41-5/6/41**LS**	22/2/46-22/3/46**HG**
4/3/42-27/3/42**LS**	27/3/47-29/4/47**LS**
17/12/42-23/1/43**LS**	21/7/47-4/9/47**LO**
11/7/43-4/9/43**LO**	9/6/48-27/8/48**HG**
17/11/43-8/1/44**HG**	13/6/49-2/8/49**HI**
13/3/45-11/4/45**HS**	5/6/50-24/6/50**LC**
	13/9/50-19/10/50**HG**

46244 KING GEORGE VI

Built Crewe 12/7/40, cost £9,290 (engine), £1,548 (tender)
Built streamlined, casing removed 4/9/47
Renumbered 6244 to 46244 week ending 28/8/48

Repairs BR

[Dates in first column are from out of traffic to return to traffic; the two 'mileage' figures represent, firstly the miles accumulated since the previous General or Intermediate and secondly (the generally lower figure) the miles run up from January 1st of the year of shopping. All are recorded as taking place at Crewe unless otherwise noted. StR=St Rollox]

Dates	Weekdays Waiting	Weekdays On Works	Mileage	'Jan 1' Mileage
24/10/50-13/11/50**NC**	2	15	nil	52,005
8/12/50-18/12/50**NC**	-	8	3,644	55,649
14/8/51-13/9/51**LI**	6	20	73,270	65,539
7/1/52-7/2/52**LC**	7	20	23,467	761
29/7/52-9/9/52**LI**	8	28	67,675	44,969
26/3/53-1/7/53**HG**	12	70	49,597	21,001
28/8/54-4/10/54**LI**	1	30	99,331	58,031
4/2/55-2/3/55**LC***	-	22	27,748	7,844
21/11/55-21/12/55**LI**	6	20	86,959	67,055
21/8/56-27/9/56**LC***	3	29	58,715	57,221
25/5/57-11/7/57**HG**	7	33	108,988	27,615
29/8/57-31/8/57**NC***	-	2	10,259	37,874
13/9/58-24/10/58**HI**	7	28	97,613	54,250
26/2/60-11/6/60**HG**	17	73	93,291	7,015

record ends
*='(EO)'- Engine Only

Sheds
Camden	13/7/40
Polmadie loan	28/9/40
Camden	19/10/40
Carlisle Upperby	14/6/58

Stored 30/12/63-2/3/64

Tenders
No	Fitted
9807	12/7/40
9808	26/6/45

Boilers
Fitted	No.	From
8/1/44	10639	6231
22/3/46	10288	6227
27/8/48	9937	6232
19/10/50	10301	6224
1/7/53	10642	-
11/7/57	10299	-
11/6/60	10644	-

No record after this date

Dog days for 46244, at Stirling shed on 17 July 1963. The engine worked north from Carlisle on the 9.30pm Sutton Coldfield to Stirling Car Sleeper. This was certainly not the oddest working of the Coronations in those last years, and it is a pity that no photographic evidence exists now of the red Coronation at Edinburgh Haymarket about 1962, off the 6.25pm Perth-Edinburgh, the overnight Inverness sleeper. Can any reader help? Though often disfigured by that terrible cabside stripe, one small saving grace of the Coronations' abrupt and early withdrawal was that it predated the nameplate fever, and none seem to have been forced to travel around with nameplates off, substituted by chalked or wooden versions. Photograph Malcolm Castledine.

Like some vast green dragon, Camden's 46245 CITY OF LONDON dozes in the sunlight dapple at Carlisle, 18 April 1955. The calm belies the ferocious heat, toil, noise and motion of a job on these engines. They had to be treated with respect; immediately in advance of certain single bore tunnels, for instance, crews would take the precaution of retreating to the cab corners, to avoid any blow-back of the fire. Photograph J. Robertson, B.P. Hoper Collection.

LMS 'Summary' *(this became 'Annual Statistics' from 1951)*

Year	Mileage	Weekdays out of service			
		wks	shed	n/req	total
1943	53,449	-	10	-	10
1944	74,751	16	81	4	101
1945	61,354	41	86	-	127
1946	79,336	35	52	2	89
1947	54,522	88	50	1	139
1948	82,821	41	36	1	78
1949	66,210	56	60	2	118
1950	79,621	52	43	-	95
1951	71,098	57	44	1	102
1952	62,552	75	50	-	125
1953	68,439	70	46	-	116
1954	73,709	58	60	-	118
1955	77,052	39	53	14	106
1956	69,182	45	100	-	145
1957	78,103	38	59	-	97
1958	86,120	-	92	-	92
1959	85,175		*record ends*		
1960	80,653				
1961	44,094				
1962	33,442				
1963	26,082				

wks=heavy and light repairs at main works
shed=shed repairs and examinations
n/req= not required

Total Recorded Mileage 1,408,315
Withdrawn week ending 12/9/64
Cut up J.Cashmore, Great Bridge 12/64

Repairs LMS

18/5/44-5/6/44**LS**	2/5/49-27/6/49**LC**
8/6/45-25/7/45**LS**	24/11/49-23/12/49**LI**
24/6/46-2/8/46**LS**	4/1/50-17/1/50**NC**
14/7/47-23/10/47**HG**	27/1/50-14/2/50**NC**
12/7/48-27/8/48**LS**	8/11/50-9/12/50**HG**
11/4/49-14/4/49**#**	**#**'No report'

46245 CITY OF LONDON

Built Crewe 26/6/43 *'built with <u>Repaired</u> boiler. For cost including NEW boiler see Engine 6246 - Total <u>including</u> £75 Patterns and £364 Sup'ter = £10,182'*
Built streamlined, casing removed 23/10/47
Renumbered 6245 to 46245 week ending 28/8/48

Repairs BR

[Dates in first column are from out of traffic to return to traffic; the two 'mileage' figures represent, firstly the miles accumulated since the previous General or Intermediate and secondly (the generally lower figure) the miles run up from January 1st of the year of shopping. All are recorded as taking place at Crewe unless otherwise noted. StR=St Rollox]

Dates	Weekdays Waiting	Weekdays On Works	Mileage	'Jan 1' Mileage
11/6/51-3/7/51**LC**	-	19	42,117	38,239
6/11/51-20/12/51**HI**	12	26	74.670	70,792
2/1/52-12/1/52**NC***	-	9	306	Nil
11/6/52-6/9/52**HI**	1	74	36,852	36,546
12/2/53-11/4/53**HG**	5	44	36,384	10,378
14/4/53-18/7/53**NC***	-	4	24	10,402
9/9/53-29/9/53**LC***	8	9	29,507	39,885
13/2/54-16/3/54**LI**	4	22	66,814	8,753
19/10/54-25/11/54**LC***	8	24	55,690	64,443
21/6/55-5/8/55**LI**	-	39	104,056	39,700
12/9/56-3/11/56**HG**	12	33	92,977	55,025
12/11/57-28/12/57**LI**	1	37	92,701	78,544
9/2/59-20/3/59**HI**	7	27	98,809	12,530
26/3/60-13/5/60**HI#**	5	35	94,518	21,873
20/3/61-15/5/61**HI**	17	30	71,223	12,443

#'boiler lifted out and put back'
record ends
*****='(EO)'- Engine Only

Sheds

Camden	26/6/43
Willesden	7/9/63

Stored 29/9/63-13/11/63

Tenders

No	Fitted
9808	26/6/43
9807	26/6/45

Boilers

Fitted	No.	From
26/6/43	9940	-
23/10/47	10306	6240
9/12/50	10287	6249
11/4/53	10290	-
3/11/56	10292	-

No record after this date

46245 CITY OF LONDON, by now in red, with The Caledonian at Euston on 29 July 1959. The nobbly-kneed spotter gapes in awe, as successive generations did. The Caledonian was a prestige train and despite its light loading (for a Coronation) could get into trouble. On one infamous occasion the train was stopped at Rugby while the crew took the engine to the shed for *extra* coal. Photograph Hamish Stevenson.

The lone 'Semi'. 46246 CITY OF MANCHESTER at Glasgow Central with The Mid-Day Scot, 18 April 1959. It had gone to Camden when new in the War but was a Crewe North engine for many years, from 1948, only returning to Camden in 1960. The engine had been painted red in October 1958, but the Polmadie and Crewe engines mostly remained green. One theory is that only LM-based engines were painted red, with the Scottish ones left green out of deference for national feeling on the independent Scottish Region. Allan Baker's is the true explanation; the original idea was to paint just sufficient engines to work the then new 'Caledonian' and this was expanded for a while. However, the Crewe and Polmadie ones tended to be engaged on night work to a much greater extent than the others, and as red was more expensive, *'somebody decided it was pointless painting engines red at greater expense if nobody was going to see them'.* Photograph James Stevenson.

46246 CITY OF MANCHESTER

Built Crewe 11/8/43, cost £10,107 (engine), £1,670 (tender)
'Built with New boiler, other three engines 6245, 6247 and 6248 being fitted, as new,
with Repaired boilers. Above cost includes <u>New</u> boiler'.
Built streamlined, casing removed 23/10/46
Renumbered 6246 to 46246 week ending 20/11/48

46246 CITY OF MANCHESTER cast in shadow, with 46223 PRINCESS ALICE in the brightness alongside, at Glasgow Central in 1958. '46' was the last to lose the 'Semi' status, getting a conventional smokebox early in 1960. There was no drive to remove the 'Semi' type smokeboxes, they were simply replaced as and when renewal of the shell or rings became necessary. Photograph J. Robertson, B.P. Hoper Collection.

Repairs LMS

14/2/44-11/3/44**TRO**	25/9/48-16/11/48**HG**
1/8/44-23/8/44**LS**	2/8/49-1/10/49**HI**
21/3/45-26/4/45**LO**	7/10/49-22/10/49**NC**
14/10/45-17/11/45**LS**	5/12/49-20/12/49**NC**
6/9/46-23/10/46**HG**	4/3/50-16/3/50**NC**
17/10/47-23/11/47**LS**	10/11/50-21/12/50**HG**

Repairs BR

[Dates in first column are from out of traffic to return to traffic; the two 'mileage' figures represent, firstly the miles accumulated since the previous General or Intermediate and secondly (the generally lower figure) the miles run up from January 1st of the year of shopping. All are recorded as taking place at Crewe unless otherwise noted. StR=St Rollox]

Dates	Weekdays Waiting	Weekdays On Works	Mileage	'Jan 1' Mileage
16/2/52-22/3/52**LI**	4	26	92,506	10,821
3/4/52-4/4/52**NC***	-	1	1,130	11,951
9/4/53-12/6/53**HG**	6	49	90,681	19,707
19/6/53-26/6/53**NC***	1	5	411	20,118
28/10/54-6/12/54**LI**	7	26	110,758	63,096
16/2/56-24/3/56**LI**	5	27	97,487	11,073
5/4/56-12/4/56**NC***	-	6	726	11,799
21/6/56-28/6/56**NC***	-	6	15,593	26,666
25/3/57-2/5/57**HG**	9	23	72,349	15,559
24/6/57-27/6/57#	-	3	-	-
8/10/57-12/10/57**NC***	2	2	31,408	46,967
23/6/58-11/7/58**NC***	4	12	88,036	37,169
2/9/58-9/10/58**LI**	6	26	99,686	48,819
20/9/59-3/10/59**NC***	1	10	71,169	58,206
11/2/60-5/4/60**HG**	-	46	97,480	8,104
15/4/61-6/6/61**HI**	7	37	89,758	21,166

#*'painting only'*
record ends
*='(EO)'- Engine Only

LMS 'Summary' *(this became 'Annual Statistics' from 1951)*

Year	Mileage	Weekdays out of service			
		wks	shed	n/req	total
1943	38,474	-	6	-	6
1944	82,091	44	44	-	88
1945	53,.457	54	92	1	147
1946	83,208	41	64	1	106
1947	65,562	35	61	1	97
1948	69,860	45	35	-	80
1949	56,866	62	54	7	123
1950	66,835	35	49	13	97
1951	81,085	-	60	1	61
1952	81,795	30	57	-	87
1953	67,369	61	51	-	112
1954	68,724	33	63	1	97
1955	80,786	-	53	17	70
1956	67,863	38	47	-	85
1957	66,426	35	44	2	81
1958	66,782	32	67	-	99
1959	71,413		*record ends*		

wks=heavy and light repairs at main works
shed=shed repairs and examinations
n/req= not required

Total Recorded Mileage 1,168,596
Withdrawn week ending 26/1/63
Cut up Crewe Works 5/63

Sheds

Camden	7/8/43
Crewe North	1/5/48
Camden	11/6/60

Stored 5/11/62-26/1/63

Tenders

No	Fitted
9809	11/8/43
9749	16/5/61

Boilers

Fitted	No.	From
23/10/46	10639	6244
16/11/48	10289	6236
21/12/50	9937	6244
12/6/53	10646	-
2/5/57	10640	-
5/4/60	9937	-

No record after this date

46247 CITY OF LIVERPOOL

Built Crewe 13/9/43, cost £8,962 (engine), £1,670 (tender)

'Built with <u>Repaired</u> boiler. For cost of engine including NEW boiler see 6246 - total <u>includes</u> £75 Patterns and £364 Superheater'.

Built streamlined, casing removed 20/6/47

Renumbered 6247 to 46247 week ending 20/11/48

46247 CITY OF LIVERPOOL on 31 May 1963, demonstrating once again that extraordinary quality of *length*, at Kingmoor almost at the very moment of withdrawal, still with nameplate and having avoided the fate of the crude stripe denoting 'banned south of Crewe'. LM express types were banned in this fashion; the overhead line clearance was tighter south of Crewe, and the bar also took in 4Fs with taller chimneys. As it was, it seems the sheds didn't take the chance and applied the stripe to 4Fs willy-nilly. Photograph Gavin Morrison.

LMS 'Summary' (this became 'Annual Statistics' from 1951)

Year	Mileage	Weekdays out of service			
		wks	shed	n/req	total
1943	23,701	-	10	-	10
1944	80,142	17	59	-	76
1945	63,870	93	45	2	140
1946	86,621	28	44	4	76
1947	47,201	68	90	4	162
1948	64,330	28	70	-	98
1949	81,092	7	75	2	84
1950	72,945	43	62	-	105
1951	73,293	37	56	1	94
1952	75,194	50	60	-	110
1953	83,445	9	70	-	79
1954	83,128	35	53	1	89
1955	79,448	29	66	8	103
1956	69,011	66	52	-	118
1957	79,416	-	80	-	80
1958	70,944	38	93	-	131
1959	60,968		*record ends*		
1960	84,439				
1961	49,906				
1962	47,830				
1963	11,263				

wks=heavy and light repairs at main works
shed=shed repairs and examinations
n/req= not required

Total Recorded Mileage 1,388,187
Withdrawn week ending 25/5/63
Cut up Crewe Works 7/63

Repairs BR

[Dates in first column are from out of traffic to return to traffic; the two 'mileage' figures represent, firstly the miles accumulated since the previous General or Intermediate and secondly (the generally lower figure) the miles run up from January 1st of the year of shopping. All are recorded as taking place at Crewe unless otherwise noted. StR=St Rollox]

Dates	Weekdays Waiting	Weekdays On Works	Mileage	'Jan 1' Mileage
6/1/51-24/1/51**HC**	-	15	72,941	nil
21/5/51-15/6/51**HG**	-	22	98,484	25,543
10/1/52-18/2/52**HC**	10	23	49,580	1,830
6/12/52-8/1/53**HI**	1	25	122,944	75,194
11/1/54-20/2/54**HG**	7	28	86,300	2,855
17/4/55-21/5/55**HI**	2	27	105,310	25,037
6/8/56-26/9/56**HG**	7	37	109,402	54,991
20/10/56-15/11/56**LC***	9	13	3,158	58,149
7/9/57-14/9/57**NC***	4	2	67,252	53,232
10/4/58-24/5/58**LI**	1	37	108,471	15,035
2/6/59-25/7/59**HG**	5	41	98,214	42,305
9/12/60-26/1/61**HI**	2	37	103,102	84,439
11/4/61-16/5/61**LC**	14	16	15,999	15,999

record ends
*='(EO)'- Engine Only

Sheds
Camden	18/9/43
Carlisle Kingmoor	6/61
Is a note 'NW 2/12/62'
Stored 22/4/63-20/5/63

Tenders
No	Fitted
9810	13/9/43
9811	13/10/44
9807	3/6/52
9749	24/12/52
9809	16/5/61

Repairs LMS
14/6/44-3/7/44**TRO**	
2/2/45-5/4/45**LS**	
1/8/45-14/9/45**LO**	
25/3/46-26/4/46**LS**	
30/4/47-20/6/47**HG**	
4/10/47-30/10/47**HO**	
14/10/48-15/11/48**HS**	
23/12/49-1/2/50**LI**	
6/2/50-17/2/50**NC**	
28/2/50-22/3/50**LC**	

Boilers
Fitted	No.	From
13/9/43	?	new
20/6/47	10293	6237
15/6/51	10289	46246
20/2/54	9937	-
26/9/56	10297	-
25/7/59	10472	-

No record after this date

Crewe North's 46248 CITY OF LEEDS. It got this name from new, a couple of years after the first CITY OF LEEDS, 6244, had been renamed KING GEORGE VI. This is 1956, and around this period, or a year or so after, 46248 was Crewe North's 'Royal'. Not least because of unpredictable Type 4 diesel failures (and the blighting effect on a career, thereby) steam was preferred on Royal Trains until about 1963; Crewe North kept a set of burnished buffers for its Royal engine, and a similarly treated set of screw couplings and drawhooks, as well as a polished set of valve and cylinder covers. The engine was hand polished to perfection and the last coal carefully placed by hand *after* a gingerly executed visit to the coaling plant. Placing a pristine locomotive under a coaler was asking for an all-over coat of dust and remonstrations from the foreman of apocalyptic proportions. Photograph J. Robertson, B.P. Hoper Collection.

46248 CITY OF LEEDS

Built Crewe 2/10/43, cost £9,370 (engine), £1,670 (tender)
'Built with <u>Repaired</u> boiler. For cost of engine including NEW boiler see 6246 - total <u>includes</u> £75 Patterns and £364 Superheater'
Built streamlined, casing removed 7/12/46
Renumbered 6248 to 46248 week ending 19/3/49

LMS 'Summary' (this became 'Annual Statistics' from 1951)

Year	Mileage	wks	shed	n/req	total
		Weekdays out of service			
1943	22,485	-	3	-	3
1944	71,367	-	101	-	101
1945	69,925	40	58	-	98
1946	74,447	53	46	3	102
1947	65,308	67	39	1	107
1948	75,991	10	59	2	71
1949	64,669	34	55	8	97
1950	60,091	29	72	10	111
1951	57,191	44	67	1	112
1952	76,168	32	52	-	84
1953	67,162	33	84	-	117
1954	80,829	-	58	1	59
1955	51,109	89	32	2	123
1956	82,662	-	54	-	54
1957	76,229	37	39	-	76
1958	73,776	36	48	1	85
1959	67,090		*record ends*		

wks=heavy and light repairs at main works
shed=shed repairs and examinations
n/req= not required

Total Recorded Mileage 1,136,499
Withdrawn week ending 5/9/64
Cut up J.Cashmore, Great Bridge 11/64

Boilers

Fitted	No.	From
2/10/43	?	new
7/12/46	10290	6224
17/3/49	10288	6244
24/3/51	10641	6235
1/10/53	10638	-
19/2/57	10304	-
22/8/59	10294	-

No record after this date

Repairs LMS

4/4/45-24/4/45	**LS**
4/12/45-10/1/46	**LS**
19/10/46-7/12/46	**HG**
30/5/47-25/6/47	**LO**
3/11/47-14/11/47	**TRO**
19/11/47-1/1/48	**HS**
14/3/48-25/3/48	**LO**
7/2/49-17/3/49	**HG**

Repairs BR

[Dates in first column are from out of traffic to return to traffic; the two 'mileage' figures represent, firstly the miles accumulated since the previous General or Intermediate and secondly (the generally lower figure) the miles run up from January 1st of the year of shopping. All are recorded as taking place at Crewe unless otherwise noted. StR=St Rollox]

Dates	Weekdays Waiting	Weekdays On Works	Mileage	'Jan 1' Mileage
6/5/50-9/6/50**LI**	1	28	74,649	16,922
26/2/51-24/3/51**HG**	2	20	50,849	7,680
31/3/51-17/4/51**NC**	-	14	349	8,029
2/6/51-12/6/51**NC**	2	6	8,283	15,963
21/7/52-27/8/52**HI**	6	26	95,289	45,778
24/8/53-1/10/53**HG**	-	33	76,441	46,051
27/5/55-2/7/55**LI**	5	26	133,882	31,942
18/8/55-7/10/55**LC***	19	24	7,236	39,178
2/11/55-19/11/55**NC***	4	11	10,148	42,090
3/10/56-9/10/56**NC***	1	4	80,136	60,969
7/1/57-19/2/57**HG**	14	23	103,495	1,666
12/10/57-18/10/57**NC***	1	4	57,670	59,336
25/4/58-6/6/58**LI**	2	34	102,515	27,852
28/6/59-22/8/59**HG**	2	45	88,116	42,192
31/8/59-16/9/59**NC***	-	14	1,080	43,272
6/9/60-20/10/60**LI**	11	27	79,258	54,340

record ends
*** = '(EO)'- Engine Only**

Sheds

Camden	2/19/43
Crewe (loan)	9/10/43
Camden	16/10/43
Crewe North	26/6/48
Carlisle Upperby	26/6/54
Crewe North	18/9/54
Camden	11/6/60
Carlisle Upperby	13/8/60
Camden	3/9/60
Crewe North	24/9/60

Stored 6/11/62-7/12/62,
24/9/63-12/12/63

Tenders

No	Fitted
9811	2/10/43
9810	13/10/44

In less than Royal condition, 46248, the classic Crewe North 'night bird' makes ready for another nocturnal return south. Polmadie, 1958; alongside is Royal Scot No.46102 BLACK WATCH. Photograph J. Robertson, B.P. Hoper Collection.

46249 CITY OF SHEFFIELD

Built Crewe 19/4/44, cost £9,994 (engine), £1,670 (tender)
Non-streamlined, built with streamlined tender
Renumbered 6249 to 46239 week ending 17/4/48

LMS 'Summary' (this became 'Annual Statistics' from 1951)

Year	Mileage	works	shed	n/req	total
		Weekdays out of service			
1944	31,778	-	43	-	43
1945	73,044	46	71	1	118
1946	78,437	19	89	2	110
1947	42,404	90	56	3	149
1948	73,389	40	35	1	76
1949	77,119	56	38	1	95
1950	81,224	35	49	-	84
1951	70,614	51	45	-	96
1952	73,702	55	53	-	108
1953	84,117	64	33	-	97
1954	73,685	37	60	-	97
1955	78,310	-	50	2	52
1956	56,019	68	33	-	101
1957	69,307	31	46	1	78
1958	71,771	36	54	-	90
1959	79,277	*record ends*			
1960	64,746				
1961	40,759				
1962	39,838				

works=heavy and light repairs at main works
shed=shed repairs and examinations
n/req= not required

Total Recorded Mileage 1,259,540
Withdrawn week ending 9/11/63
Cut up Crewe Works 12/63

Repairs LMS

1/8/45-22/9/45**LS**	17/5/48-27/5/48**TRO**
29/8/46-19/9/46**LS**	18/10/48-28/10/48**LO**
23/4/47-29/5/47**LO**	2/12/48-6/1/49**HI**
30/8/47-5/11/47**HG**	28/9/49-19/11/49**LI**
13/4/48-15/4/48**NC**	17/8/50-27/9/50**HG**
23/4/48-23/4/48**NC**	23/7/51-23/8/51**HI**

Repairs BR

[Dates in first column are from out of traffic to return to traffic; the two 'mileage' figures represent, firstly the miles accumulated since the previous General or Intermediate and secondly (the generally lower figure) the miles run up from January 1st of the year of shopping. All are recorded as taking place at Crewe unless otherwise noted. StR=St Rollox]

Dates	Weekdays Waiting	Weekdays On Works	Mileage	'Jan 1' Mileage
14/11/51-12/12/51**LC**	8	16	21,313	67,181
18/6/52-2/8/52**LI**	7	34	66,924	42,178
10/12/52-3/2/53**HG**	5	40	31,524	73,702
25/2/53-9/3/53**NC***	-	10	nil	nil
23/9/53-20/10/53**HC**	6	17	63,052	63,052
19/8/54-1/10/54**HG**	3	34	140,568	55,851
13/1/56-27/2/56**LI**	2	36	97,263	1,119
13/10/56-11/11/56**LC***	7	23	49,560	50,679
26/7/57-31/8/57**HG**	2	29	96,291	41,391
13/11/58-17/1/59**LI**	4	50	99,687	71,771
22/2/60-27/4/60**HG**	1	54	91,130	11,853
4/1/62-9/2/62**HI**	-	31	93,681	29

record ends
*='(EO)'- Engine Only

Sheds
Crewe North	22/4/44
Polmadie (loan)	8/7/44
Polmadie	26/8/44
Crewe North (loan)	14/10/44
Polmadie	11/11/44
Carlisle Upperby (loan)	12/10/46
Carlisle Upperby	2/11/46
Camden	28/5/49
Crewe North	20/11/54
Polmadie (loan)	11/3/61
Polmadie	1/4/61

Tenders
No	Fitted
9812	19/4/44
9749	23/1/45
9743	9/8/45

Boilers

Fitted	No.	From
5/11/47	10287	6222
27/9/50	12472	6255
3/2/53	10645	-
1/10/54	10639	-
31/8/57	10296	-
27/4/60	10293	-

No record after this date

46249 CITY OF SHEFFIELD completely dwarfing Compound 4-4-0 No.41103—an engine built for LMS express work not much more than a decade before the first Coronation appeared, it can be mused. Carlisle Citadel, 23 April 1953. Photograph James Stevenson.

LMS 'Summary' (this became 'Annual Statistics' from 1951)

Year	Mileage	Weekdays out of service			
		works	shed	n/req	total
1944	51,185	-	20	8	28
1945	90,429	35	51	4	90
1946	72,874	46	79	1	126
1947	47,730	114	35	2	151
1948	73,104	-	72	-	72
1949	62,915	41	70	3	114
1950	63,003	80	32	-	112
1951	68,363	64	62	1	127
1952	79,494	57	39	-	96
1953	84,501	18	75	-	93
1954	71,712	30	89	-	119
1955	79,730	30	59	10	99
1956	78,578	37	65	-	102
1957	74,155	49	57	-	106
1958	73,640	26	77	1	104
1959	61,233		record ends		
1960	74,142				
1962	47,997				
1963	31,381				

works=heavy and light repairs at main works
shed=shed repairs and examinations
n/req= not required

Total Recorded Mileage 1,353,526
Withdrawn week ending 12/9/64
Cut up West of Scotland
Shipbreaking Co, Troon 12/64

Repairs LMS

27/2/45-7/4/45**LS**
1/2/46-28/2/46**LS**
1/10/46-25/10/46**LO**
16/5/47-25/9/47**HG**
22/1/49-25/2/49**HI**
1/3/49-15/3/49**NC**
21/3/49-31/3/49**HG**
23/3/50-1/5/50**HG**

Euston, 8 January 1958 and a sparkling green 46250 CITY OF LICHFIELD backs out of the terminus, bound for Camden. Photograph John Edgington.

46250 CITY OF LICHFIELD

Built Crewe 20/5/44, engine £9,994, tender £1,670
Non-streamlined, built with streamlined tender
Renumbered 6250 to 46250 week ending 26/2/49

Repairs BR

[Dates in first column are from out of traffic to return to traffic; the two 'mileage' figures represent, firstly the miles accumulated since the previous General or Intermediate and secondly (the generally lower figure) the miles run up from January 1st of the year of shopping. All are recorded as taking place at Crewe unless otherwise noted. StR=St Rollox]

Dates	Weekdays Waiting	Weekdays On Works	Mileage	'Jan 1' Mileage
6/5/50-29/5/50**LC**	3	16	396	18,098
15/11/50-15/12/50**LC**	4	22	42,550	60,252
26/9/51-3/11/51**HI**	11	22	112,854	67,553
8/11/51-14/12/51**LC***	3	28	198	67,751
5/5/52-31/5/52**LC***	-	23	31,944	31,134
18/9/52-28/10/52**HG**	6	28	65,399	64,589
11/12/53-16/1/54**LI**	8	21	99,406	84,501
11/3/54-2/4/54**LC***	5	14	9,846	9,846
10/4/55-10/5/55**HI**	1	29	93,656	21,945
12/7/56-24/8/56**HG**	4	33	106,228	48,443
3/4/57-10/4/57**NC***	-	6	53,051	22,916
19/8/57-22/8/57**NC***	1	2	85,541	55,406
21/10/57-30/11/57**HG**	1	34	101,958	71,823
2/12/57-7/12/57**NC***	-	5	-	-
10/12/57-20/12/57**NC***	-	9	-	-
21/1/58-20/2/58**LC***	13	13	7,657	5,325
2/5/59-12/6/59**LI**	4	31	101,164	25,192
5/11/59-4/12/59**LC**	-	25	31,897	57,089
2/12/60-27/1/61**HG**	10	36	74,142	74,142

record ends
*='(EO)'- Engine Only

Sheds

Crewe North	20/5/44
Polmadie (loan)	22/7/44
Polmadie	26/8/44
Carlisle Upperby (loan)	12/10/46
Carlisle Upperby	2/11/46
Camden	28/5/49
Edge Hill	30/6/56
Camden	21/7/56
Carlisle Upperby	8/9/56
Camden	20/10/56
Carlisle Upperby	14/6/58

Stored 2/1/64-17/2/64

Tenders
9813   20/5/44

Boilers

Fitted	No.	From
25/9/47	10303	6247
1/5/50	10291	6240
28/10/52	10303	-
24/8/56	9939	-
30/11/57	9938	-
27/1/61	10300	-

46251 CITY OF NOTTINGHAM, on a Crewe - Shrewsbury local, toodling through the fields and woods; the view is notable for the wisp of exhaust from the coal pusher at the rear of the tender. Such a working might well be a running in turn or, at this late time, simply a job for a spare engine; whatever, there was a very clever filling in arrangement in operation at Crewe North. The details that follow are from Baker and Morrison's *Crewe Sheds* (Ian Allan, 1988). Because they were too big for the Crewe North turntable (however bizarre it seems now — a 70ft 'table finally went in about 1950), on arrival at Crewe on up trains from Scotland, they were handed over to a set of shed men who would take the engine to the North shed for fire cleaning and whatever might be needed. Without turning, the engines were then put to work on west of England trains (such as the Liverpool to Plymouth and the Manchester - Penzance, both of which left Crewe in the middle of the morning) as far as Shrewsbury. Once there, the Coronation was replaced by a WR engine and proceeded to turn on the Severn Bridge triangle. It was then right way round to await the afternoon down west of England train and take it back to Crewe. Once 'back home' like this, they were the right way round to head north to Scotland again after servicing that evening. These filling in turns were 'nice easy footplate jobs, with several hours to spare at Shrewsbury'. Photograph B.P. Hoper Collection.

46251 CITY OF NOTTINGHAM

Built Crewe 3/6/44 cost £9,994 (engine), £1,670 (tender)
Non-streamlined, built with streamlined tender
Renumbered 6251 to 46251 week ending 29/5/48

Boilers		
Fitted	No.	From
7/8/47	10642	6227
19/5/49	10300	6234
23/11/51	10288	-
22/2/55	9938	-
21/9/57	10642	-
4/11/60	10295	-
No record after this date		

Repairs LMS
28/6/45-18/8/45**LS**
21/7/46-17/3/46**LS**
7/5/47-7/8/47**HG**
21/8/47-24/9/47**LO**
2/10/47-11/10/47**NC**
17/4/48-23/5/48**LS**
30/3/49-19/5/49**HG**

Red 46251 CITY OF NOTTINGHAM with a Crewe to Shrewsbury stopping train pulls into the bay at Shrewsbury, awaiting access to the multi-directional platform on the eastern side of the station, 15 August 1963. '51' was the engine involved in the terrible Winsford smash of 1948; 6207 was stopped by an illicit pull on the communication cord and 6251, by a signalling error, was admitted behind. The collision cost 24 lives. Photograph F.W. Shuttleworth.

Repairs BR

[Dates in first column are from out of traffic to return to traffic; the two 'mileage' figures represent, firstly the miles accumulated since the previous General or Intermediate and secondly (the generally lower figure) the miles run up from January 1st of the year of shopping. All are recorded as taking place at Crewe unless otherwise noted. StR=St Rollox]

Dates	Weekdays Waiting	Weekdays On Works	Mileage	'Jan 1' Mileage
6/6/50-21/7/50**LI**	5	34	85,930	32,946
27/11/50-30/12/50**NC**	12	16	32,351	65,297
22/10/51-23/11/51**HG**	1	27	87,408	55,057
4/1/53-6/2/53**LI**	2	26	79,075	144
8/12/53-9/1/54**HI**	5	21	58,540	58,684
22/12/54-22/2/55**HG**	8	43	66,051	66,051
8/5/56-16/6/56**HI**	6	28	94,664	25,284
3/8/57-21/9/57**HG**	9	33	85,674	45,740
18/10/58-22/11/58**HI**	2	28	90,235	70,002
14/8/59-25/9/59**LI**	9	27	54,812	48,127
4/8/60-4/11/60**HG**	10	69	70,900	49,481
record ends				

*='(EO)'- Engine Only

Sheds

Crewe North	3/6/44
Polmadie (loan)	8/7/44
Polmadie	26/8/44
Carlisle Upperby (loan)	12/10/46
Carlisle Upperby	2/11/46
Camden	26/6/48
Edge Hill	2/10/48
Crewe North	11/12/48
Camden	28/5/49
Carlisle Upperby	1/10/49
Camden	10/6/50
Carlisle Upperby	30/9/50
Edge Hill	13/3/54
Carlisle Upperby	17/4/54
Camden	18/9/54
Edge Hill	2/10/54
Camden	23/4/55

Edge Hill	21/5/55
Carlisle	18/6/55
Edge Hill	17/9/55
Carlisle Upperby	9/6/56
Crewe North	15/9/56
Carlisle Upperby	29/9/56
Crewe North	20/10/56
Carlisle Upperby	22/6/57
Crewe North	21/9/57
Camden	9/3/63
Crewe North	20/4/63

Stored 6/11/62-6/12/62, 6/10/63-12/12/63

Tenders

No	Fitted
9814	3/6/44

LMS 'Summary' (this became 'Annual Statistics' from 1951)

Year	Mileage	Weekdays out of service			
		wks	shed	n/req	total
1944	57,779	-	21	4	25
1945	63,573	45	64	10	119
1946	72,817	19	64	2	85
1947	43,154	119	34	3	156
1948	78,403	36	41	-	77
1949	69,001	43	48	6	97
1950	65,297	33	64	4	107
1951	61,776	28	60	3	91
1952	72,212	-	69	5	74
1953	58,684	49	64	10	123
1954	66,051	13	73	1	87
1955	69,380	43	49	2	94
1956	65,209	34	67	-	101
1957	65,982	42	48	-	90
1958	76,687	30	48	-	78
1959	69,546	*record ends*			
1960	60,541				
1961	57,044				
1962	34,250				
1963	29,160				

wks=heavy and light repairs at main works
shed=shed repairs and examinations
n/req= not required

Total Recorded Mileage 1,236,546
Withdrawn week ending 12/9/64
Cut up J.Cashmore, Great Bridge 12/64

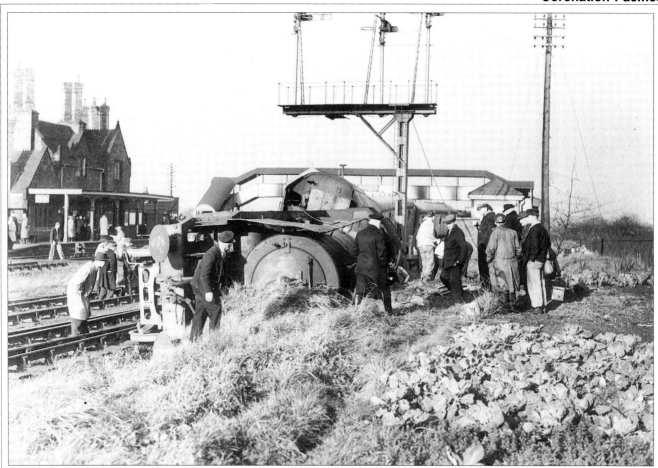

CITY OF LEICESTER came to shuddering grief, toppling over at the last, at Polesworth on 19 November 1951. The train was an up express from Glasgow, having left there at 10.30 the previous evening. It had to be diverted onto the slow because a signal was out of order but the Driver did not see the Distant, which was at caution. He braked on seeing the Home at danger but the train still passed through the crossover at 55mph, far too fast. 46252 struck the platform, which slowed it and kept it upright for longer than would have otherwise been the case. It was derailed with the eight leading coaches. The engine only toppled to its left (leaving the tender upright) after it had lost a lot of its momentum. It sustained considerable damage (as did the stock) from striking the platform faces but this was probably the train's salvation; it was slowed down sharply (and, in the event, safely!) and nobody was seriously injured.

46252 CITY OF LEICESTER

Built Crewe 26/4/44 cost £9,994 (engine), £1,670 (tender)
Non-streamlined, built with streamlined tender
Renumbered 6252 to 46252 week ending 9/4/49

46252 CITY OF LEICESTER waiting to leave Euston with the down Mid-Day Scot, 2 October 1953. Photograph Philip J. Kelley.

Repairs BR

[Dates in first column are from out of traffic to return to traffic; the two 'mileage' figures represent, firstly the miles accumulated since the previous General or Intermediate and secondly (the generally lower figure) the miles run up from January 1st of the year of shopping. All are recorded as taking place at Crewe unless otherwise noted. StR=St Rollox]

Dates	Weekdays Waiting	Weekdays On Works	Mileage	'Jan 1' Mileage
29/3/50-27/4/50**LI**	-	24	71,622	16,978
17/11/50-22/12/50**LC**	8	22	53,201	70,179
9/8/51-1/9/51**LI**	-	20	98,272	44,626
12/9/51-26/9/51**NC***	1	11	577	45,203
19/11/51-29/1/52**HG**	12	47	14,424	59,050
16/12/52-13/2/54**HI**	3	28	72,105	72,105
10/1/54-23/1/53**HG**	4	25	69,608	1,886
14/5/55-11/6/55**LI**	1	23	106,699	27,066
15/12/56-26/1/57**HG**	1	33	116,387	64,297
22/10/57-26/10/57**NC***	2	2	59,381	59,381
28/2/58-18/4/58**HI**	4	37	79,546	8,800
7/1/59-13/2/59**HI**	4	28	61,326	2,338
16/3/59-2/4/59**LC***	4	14	4,572	6,910
16/12/59-5/2/60**HG**	9	33	65,490	67,828
28/8/61-2/10/61**LI**	-	30	108,904	35,391

record ends
*='(EO)'- Engine Only

Sheds

Crewe North	24/6/44
Camden	10/6/50
Crewe North	30/9/50
Camden	10/2/51
Crewe North	24/3/51
Camden	10/11/51
Crewe North	12/1/52
Camden	5/7/52
Crewe North	20/9/52
Carlisle Upperby	13/6/53
Crewe North	19/9/53
Carlisle Upperby	9/6/56
Crewe North	15/9/56
Carlisle Upperby	11/6/60
Camden	22/9/62

Stored 18/11/62-31/5/63

Tenders

No	Fitted
9815	24/6/44

Boilers

Fitted	No.	From
7/12/46	10645	6246
1/11/47	10295	6228
7/4/49	10639	6246
29/1/52	9939	-
13/2/54	10641	-
26/1/57	10303	-
5/2/60		10304

No record after this date

Repairs LMS

9/2/45-9/3/45**LO**
29/9/45-1/11/45**LS**
28/1/46-5/3/46**LO**
9/11/46-7/12/46**HG**
21/5/47-23/6/47**LO**
23/9/47-1/11/47**HS**
2/3/49-7/4/49**HG**

LMS 'Summary' *(this became 'Annual Statistics' from 1951)*

Year	Mileage	Weekdays out of service			
		wks	shed	n/req	total
1944	41,945	-	12	4	16
1945	57,376	54	46	4	104
1946	60,433	57	49	-	106
1947	62,427	64	30	1	95
1948	72,475	-	64	1	65
1949	63,236	32	46	11	89
1950	70,624	54	24	3	81
1951	59,050	66	44	2	112
1952	72,105	34	68	1	103
1953	67,881	22	64	3	89
1954	81,519	29	29	2	60
1955	79,156	24	24	4	52
1956	64,297	11	77	1	89
1957	70,746	23	54	1	78
1958	67,788	41	44	1	86
1959	67,828		*record ends*		
1960	73,613				
1961	50,880				
1962	47,653				
1963					

wks=heavy and light repairs at main works
shed=shed repairs and examinations
n/req= not required

Total Recorded Mileage 1,231,032
Withdrawn week ending 1/6/63
Cut up Crewe Works 9/63

46253 CITY OF ST ALBANS at Carlisle (during the removal of the lovely ecclesiastical end screen), 30 August 1958. A curious little feature of the nameplate was that the small T in St Albans was raised, and underlined. Photograph W. Hermiston, B.P. Hoper Collection.

LMS 'Summary' *(this became 'Annual Statistics' from 1951)*

Year	Mileage	Weekdays out of service			
		wks	shed	n/req	total
1946	24,208	-	11	5	16
1947	74,881	8	62	2	72
1948	60,660	28	102	-	130
1949	58,595	51	30	5	86
1950	77,337	-	80	4	84
1951	56,674	42	70	5	117
1952	60,056	31	76	6	113
1953	82,427	35	55	-	90
1954	91,086	7	56	1	64
1955	54,140	97	64	3	164
1956	81,256	35	75	-	110
1957	69,797	20	57	-	77
1958	75,214	23	57	-	80
1959	65,086		record ends		

wks=heavy and light repairs at main works
shed=shed repairs and examinations
n/req= not required
Total Recorded Mileage 931,417
Withdrawn week ending 26/1/63
'Date actually broken up
Crewe Works 13/5/63'

Boilers

Fitted	No.	From
14/9/46	12470	new
17/2/51	10296	6222
26/11/53	12471	-
3/12/55	13043	-
25/1/58	10300	-
2/6/60	13043	-
No record after this date		

46253 CITY OF ST ALBANS

Built Crewe 14/9/46 total cost £15,460
Built without streamlining
Renumbered 6253 to 46253 week ending 17/9/49

Repairs BR

[Dates in first column are from out of traffic to return to traffic; the two 'mileage' figures represent, firstly the miles accumulated since the previous General or Intermediate and secondly (the generally lower figure) the miles run up from January 1st of the year of shopping. All are recorded as taking place at Crewe unless otherwise noted. StR=St Rollox]

Dates	Weekdays Waiting	Weekdays On Works	Mileage	'Jan 1' Mileage
13/8/47-14/8/47**NC**	-	2	73,866	49,658
3/10/47-11/10/47**TRO**	-	8#	-	-
11/12/47-19/12/47**NC**	-	8	96,574	72,366
28/1/48-28/2/48**LS**	-	28	105,163	6,074
25/3/48-15/4/48**NC**	-	18	3,169	9,243
29/11/48-22/12/48**NC**	-	21	53,554	59,628
22/7/49-14/9/49**LI**	-	47	94,135	39,549
19/9/49-22/9/49**NC**	-	4	175	39,724
17/3/50-31/3/50**NC**	8	4	35,019	15,973
1/1/51-17/2/51**HG**	5	36	96,525	142
27/6/51-28/6/51**LC**	-	1	22,308	22,450
24/4/52-30/5/52**HI**	3	28	74,919	18,387
5/6/53-9/6/53**LC***	-	3#	81,121	39,452
20/10/53-26/11/53**HG**	6	26	115,466	73,797
16/12/54-24/12/54**LC**	1	6	98,612	89,982
18/4/55-19/4/55**LC**	-	1	101,798	2,082
2/3/55-23/4/55**LI**	6	42	110,925	11,209
8/10/55-3/12/55**HC***	9	39	37,728	48,937
3/9/56-13/10/56**HI**	6	29	108,896	65,965
21/8/57-26/8/57**NC***	1	3	63,284	47,993
12/12/57-25/1/58**HG**	8	35	85,088	69,797
31/4/59-8/5/59**LI**	1	32	90,474	15,260
19/4/60-2/6/60**HG**	5	33	73,532	22,706
20/1/61-25/2/61**LC**	2	29	51,826	2,765

#'shed'
record ends
='(EO)'- Engine Only*

Sheds

Camden	14/9/46
Carlisle Upperby (loan)	22/1/49
Camden	23/7/49
Carlisle Upperby	1/10/49
Camden	10/6/50
Carlisle Upperby	30/9/50
Crewe North	20/9/52
Camden (loan)	11/10/52
Camden	27/6/53
Crewe North	21/9/57
Stored 3/10/62-26/1/63	

Tenders

No	Fitted
9816	14/9/46
9703	28/6/51
9816	1/9/51
9750	24/12/54
9816	19/1/55
9704	?

CITY OF ST ALBANS in slightly hybrid state at Crewe, 11 September 1949. The engine, new three years before, has just completed a Light Intermediate in this view and someone has yet to sort out the new smokebox numberplate. This was fitted in the next day or so. Photograph John Edgington.

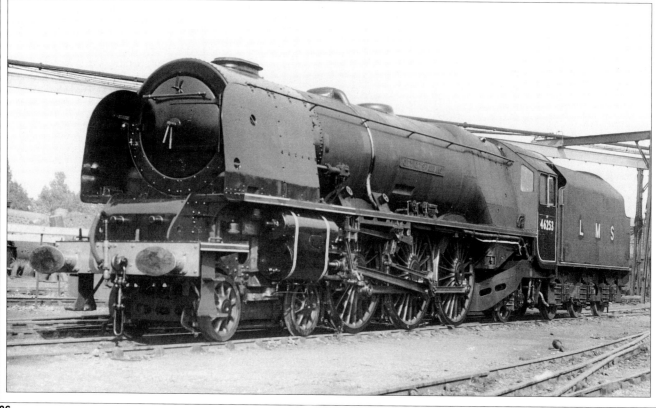

46254 CITY OF STOKE-ON-TRENT

Built Crewe 17/9/46, total cost £15,460
Built without streamlining
Renumbered 6254 to 46254 week ending 23/7/49

46254 CITY OF STOKE-ON-TRENT after arrival at Euston with The Ulster Express, 27 September 1958. This engine, it was, that provided the author's first view of a fabled 'Duchess', from the little footbridge leading into Camden shed. The first meeting with a 'big 'un' seems to live on in most observer's minds and I return yet again to the themes of power, size, majesty and all the rest. It has to be said, there was nothing quite like them. In the last six, 46252-46257, there was a departure from the welded tenders; the riveting is just visible in the feeble light of Old Euston. Photograph B.P. Hoper Collection.

Repairs BR

[Dates in first column are from out of traffic to return to traffic; the two 'mileage' figures represent, firstly the miles accumulated since the previous General or Intermediate and secondly (the generally lower figure) the miles run up from January 1st of the year of shopping. All are recorded as taking place at Crewe unless otherwise noted. StR=St Rollox]

Dates	Weekdays Waiting	Weekdays On Works	Mileage	'Jan 1' Mileage
25/11/50-8/12/50**NC**	1	10	16,545	53,883
14/2/51-19/3/51**LC**	10	18	32,181	10,093
13/9/51-15/10/51**HI**	-	27	71,890	49,802
11/1/53-21/2/53**HG**	-	35	75,332	543
11/6/53-1/7/53**LC***	4	13	21,521	22,064
10/6/54-28/7/54**HI**	-	41	94,349	33,781
13/9/55-18/10/55**HG**	1	29	99,270	60,022
11/3/57-17/4/57**HG**	2	30	116,251	10,770
27/9/57-9/10/57**NC***	8	2	35,683	46,453
11/7/58-8/9/58**LI**	13	26	99,126	42,028
5/12/58-10/1/59**LC***	8	21	24,681	66,709
15/8/59-16/10/59**HI**	21	32	82,304	57,623
25/5/60-16/6/60**LC***	-	19	41,729	25,722
2/3/61-25/4/61**HG**	10	35	90,380	9,834

record ends
*=‘(EO)’- Engine Only

Sheds

Camden	21/9/46
Carlisle Upperby	1/10/49
Crewe North	20/9/52
Camden (loan)	11/10/52
Crewe North	25/10/52
Carlisle Upperby	13/6/53
Camden	19/9/53
Edge Hill	22/1/55
Camden	5/2/55
Western Region	28/1/56
Camden	25/2/56
Crewe North	24/9/60
Camden	9/3/63
Crewe North	20/4/63

Stored 3/10/62-3/1/63, 21/10/63-17/11/63

Tenders

No	Fitted
9817	17/9/46

Boilers

Fitted	No.	From
17/9/46	12471	new
2/9/50	10646	6233
21/2/53	13043	-
18/10/55	10305	-
17/4/57	12471	-
25/4/61	10642	-

No record after this date

Repairs LMS

8/10/47-10/10/47**NC**
19/2/47-24/12/47**NC**
16/1/48-18/3/48**LS**
10/6/49-22/7/49**HI**
16/1/50-1/2/50**NC**
19/7/50-2/9/50**HG**

LMS 'Summary' *(this became 'Annual Statistics' from 1951)*

Year	Mileage	Weekdays out of service			
		wks	shed	n/req	total
1946	25,790	-	9	1	10
1947	72,941	-	85	-	85
1948	69,115	54	48	2	104
1949	66,897	37	69	5	111
1950	59,426	39	74	2	115
1951	67,836	55	36	1	92
1952	56,755	-	94	4	98
1953	61,111	52	71	4	127
1954	73,029	41	60	-	101
1955	79,522	30	60	12	102
1956	85,981#	-	70	-	70
1957	67,868	32	65	-	97
1958	66,709	57	63	-	120
1959	73,630		*record ends*		
1960	64,539				
1961	47,086				
1962	38,724				
1963	26,082				

#'Includes miles run whilst on loan to Western Region'
wks=heavy and light repairs at main works
shed=shed repairs and examinations
n/req= not required

Total Recorded Mileage 1,103,041
Withdrawn week ending 12/9/64
Cut up J.Cashmore, Great Bridge 12/64

LMS 'Summary' (this became 'Annual Statistics' from 1951)

Year	Mileage	Weekdays out of service			
		wks	shed	n/req	total
1946	19,374	-	5	-	5
1947	75,613	17	58	-	75
1948	76,897	26	63	-	89
1949	50,233	116	39	3	158
1950	47,131	88	52	3	148
1951	53,521	86	38	3	127
1952	67,653	28	58	-	86
1953	67,306	66	54	6	126
1954	48,475	87	42	9	138
1955	71,414	-	86	8	94
1956	61,544	67	49	9	125
1957	58,240	64	38	15	117
1958	67,325	40	57	2	99
1959	62,100			record ends	

wks=heavy and light repairs at main works
shed=shed repairs and examinations
n/req= not required

Total Recorded Mileage 826,826
Withdrawn week ending 12/9/64
Cut up West of Scotland
Shipbreaking Co, Troon 12/64

Repairs LMS
25/8/47-12/9/47**LO**
29/12/47-27/1/48**HS**
8/3/49-24/6/49**LI**
25/10/49-19/11/49**LC**
2/6/50-11/8/50**HG**

Though the Coronations had long been shedded at Upperby, it was only in the first part of 1961, as the traditional allocation structure wavered before the Type 4 diesels, that some found their way to the ex-Caledonian shed at Kingmoor. Still in glorious green, this is 46255 CITY OF HEREFORD at its new home, Kingmoor, about 1963. The Record Card makes no mention of this transfer, ending with the engine's transfer to Upperby in 1956. Photograph B. Richardson, B.P. Hoper Collection.

46255 CITY OF HEREFORD

Built Crewe 16/10/46 total cost £15,460
Built without streamlining
Renumbered 6255 to 46255 week ending 25/6/49

Repairs BR

[Dates in first column are from out of traffic to return to traffic; the two 'mileage' figures represent, firstly the miles accumulated since the previous General or Intermediate and secondly (the generally lower figure) the miles run up from January 1st of the year of shopping. All are recorded as taking place at Crewe unless otherwise noted. StR=St Rollox]

Dates	Weekdays Waiting	Weekdays On Works	Mileage	'Jan 1' Mileage
23/8/50-30/8/50**NC**	-	6	293	29,516
3/10/50-4/11/50**LC**	7	21	7,407	36,630
26/2/51-6/4/51**LC**	7	26	29,406	11,498
13/4/51-12/5/59**HC**	10	15	30,217	12,309
25/10/51-27/11/51**LI**	2	26	67,126	49,218
24/11/52-15/1/53**HG**	1	42	71,956	67,653
30/10/53-24/12/53**HC***	9	38	66,951	66,951
30/12/53-12/1/54**NC***	-	11	67,306	67,306
30/7/54-9/9/54**LI**	6	29	104,365	37,059
28/10/54-20/12/54**HC***	4	41	9,919	46,978
16/2/56-3/4/56**HI**	6	33	92,111	9,281
17/9/56-19/10/56**HC***	10	18	37,875	47,156
1/12/56-10/12/56**NC***	1	6	46,995	56,276
28/8/57-2/11/57**HG**	31	33	108,094	55,831
28/7/58-23/8/58**LC***	17	23	51,497	39,088
12/4/59-23/5/59**LI**	6	29	104,150	24,396
9/6/60-17/8/60**HI**	11	48	71,237	33,521

record ends
='(EO)'- Engine Only*

Sheds

Camden	19/10/46
Carlisle Upperby	26/6/48
Crewe North	20/9/52
Carlisle Upperby	13/6/53
Camden	26/9/53
Carlisle Upperby	3/10/53
Edge Hill	21/1/56
Camden	28/1/56
Carlisle Upperby	25/2/56
Stored 1/1/64-27/1/64	

Tenders

No	Fitted
10622	16/10/46

Boilers

Fitted	No.	From
16/10/46	12472	new
11/8/50	10294	6221
15/1/53	10291	-
20/12/54	10300	-
2/11/57	10305	-
No record after this date		

46255 CITY OF HEREFORD, beautiful in its BR blue at Crewe North on 4 September 1950, rivets prominent on the tender. 46224 PRINCESS ALEXANDRA stands in the background. The 'big 'uns', indeed, spent much of the daylight 'standing around'. The Royal Scot and The Mid-Day Scot, along with the Caledonian later on, and one or two other trains, kept maybe a third of the class busy during daylight but the remainder were resting at Crewe, Polmadie, Camden and Perth.

46256 SIR WILLIAM A STANIER FRS passes through Strathbungo Junction as it leaves Glasgow Central with summer Saturday 9.55am to Euston via Kilmarnock, 1 September 1962. Photograph W.A.C. Smith.

46256 SIR WILLIAM A STANIER FRS at Camden, luxuriating in the evening sunshine and with that mountain of coal on board, ready to back down to Euston for a working north — the apparatus behind the smoke deflector is the short-lived steam turbo generator for the electric lights. The picture is full of expectancy, a foretaste of the night ahead. Oh to be on a sleeper behind one of these creatures of the night! Taken effortlessly into sleep by the drumming of the rails and the perfectly even exhaust, looking forward to daylight on some Scottish moor, and wondering which other 'big 'un' had been put on at Crewe in the darkness... Photograph Alec Swain/B.P. Hoper Collection.

Black from new, 46256 SIR WILLIAM A STANIER FRS in early 1948, a '4' hurriedly and somewhat imperfectly applied to the cab's 6256. The LM smokebox numbers were given the additional 40,000 in the traditional serif style which soon gave way to the plainer BR Gill Sans. The prominent rod emerging from the Driver's side is the modified arrangement of reversing screw of the last two engines, worked by universal joints from a handwheel to the Driver's side rather than at the front, easing its working. On all the earlier Coronations the reverser was tucked away more or less invisible, up underneath the running plate. Photograph W. Hermiston, B.P. Hoper Collection.

LMS 'Summary' *(this became 'Annual Statistics' from 1951)*

Year	Mileage	Weekdays out of service			
		wks	shed	n/req	total
1947	863	-	4	1	5
1948	48,686	-	170	-	170
1949	88,219	20	80	2	102
1950	61,412	82	73	-	155
1951	66,148	54	66	2	122
1952	71,572	43	72	-	115
1953	82,853	28	58	-	86
1954	70,352	43	70	-	113
1955	80,878	25	53	11	89
1956	66,667	45	71	-	116
1957	71,232	23	86	-	109
1958	75,385	53	46	-	93
1959	58,417		record ends		
1960	65,087				
1961	57,029				
1962	24,375				
1963	26,380				

wks=heavy and light repairs at main works
shed=shed repairs and examinations
n/req= not required

Total Recorded Mileage 1,016,060
Withdrawn week ending 3/10/64
Cut up J.Cashmore, Great Bridge 12/64

Boilers

Fitted	No.	From
13/12/47	12473	new
5/5/51	13044	new
22/6/54	12474	-
15/12/56	12473	-
15/8/59	13044	-
No record after this date		

46256 SIR WILLIAM A STANIER F.R.S.

Built Crewe 13/12/47 cost £18,248 (engine), £3,163 (tender)
Built without streamlining
Renumbered 6256 to 46256 week ending 15/5/48

Repairs BR

[Dates in first column are from out of traffic to return to traffic; the two 'mileage' figures represent, firstly the miles accumulated since the previous General or Intermediate and secondly the generally lower figure) the miles run up from January 1st of the year of shopping. All are recorded as taking place at Crewe unless otherwise noted. StR=St Rollox]

Dates	Weekdays Waiting	Weekdays On Works	Mileage	'Jan 1' Mileage
16/2/48-13/5/48NC	-	75	9,952	9,089
8/6/48-3/7/48NC	-	23	12,733	11,870
6/9/48-25/9/48NC	-	18	30,274	29,411
9/10/48-16/10/48NC	-	7	31,705	30,842
2/5/49-24/5/49HC	-	20	83,038	33,489
22/9/49-15/10/49NC	-	21	119,627	70,078
16/1/50-27/2/50LI	-	36	140,568	2,800
9/10/50-1/12/50LC	1	45	51,753	54,553
2/3/51-5/5/51HG	9	45	65,326	6,714
25/4/52-7/6/52HI	7	30	79,909	20,475
9/6/52-16/6/52NC*	-	6	Nil	20,475
26/5/53-25/6/53HC	8	18	89,863	38,766
1/7/53-3/7/53NC*	1	1	90,204	39,107
3/5/54-22/6/54HG	1	42	156,065	22,115
2/8/55-31/8/55LI	1	24	95,647	45,412
245/10/56-15/12/56HG	7	38	100,590	65,129
7/1/57-2/2/57LC*	12	11	2,393	855
25/3/58-27/5/58LI	-	53	93,594	20,824
8/6/59-15/8/59HG	1	59	89,691	35,130
5/11/60-5/1/61LI	14	36	88,073	65,087

record ends
*='(EO)'- Engine Only

Sheds

Crewe North	13/12/47
Camden	24/1/48
Crewe North	7/11/59#
Camden	7/11/59#
Crewe North	21/11/59#
Carlisle Upperby	21/11/59#
Camden	30/4/60
Crewe North	24/9/60

#same dates-no explanation
Stored 21/10/62-20/1/63, 10/10/63-2/12/63

Tenders

No	Fitted
10623	13/12/47

46256 SIR WILLIAM A STANIER FRS gets a look-over at Rugby, 4 October 1962. Few were prepared for the suddenness of the end when it came. In this year, 1962, they had even begun to appear on freight trains, and three Polmadie engines were actually withdrawn at the end of the year. The EE Type 4s, which nowhere seemed able to demonstrate any obvious superiority, had long overcome their early unreliability and were powering the best trains along the length of the West Coast. There had been talk of transferring surplus Pacifics to the workings between Glasgow and Liverpool and Manchester, and even the Southern, but this did not come about. The traditional allocation of the Coronations had been Camden, Polmadie, Upperby and Crewe North and 1961 saw the beginnings of a breakdown in this long tradition. Edge Hill, which had had them sporadically earlier on, began to get them, then Kingmoor and then Willesden. Soon they were best noted for heroic episodes deputising for failed Type 4s. Photograph B.P. Hoper Collection.

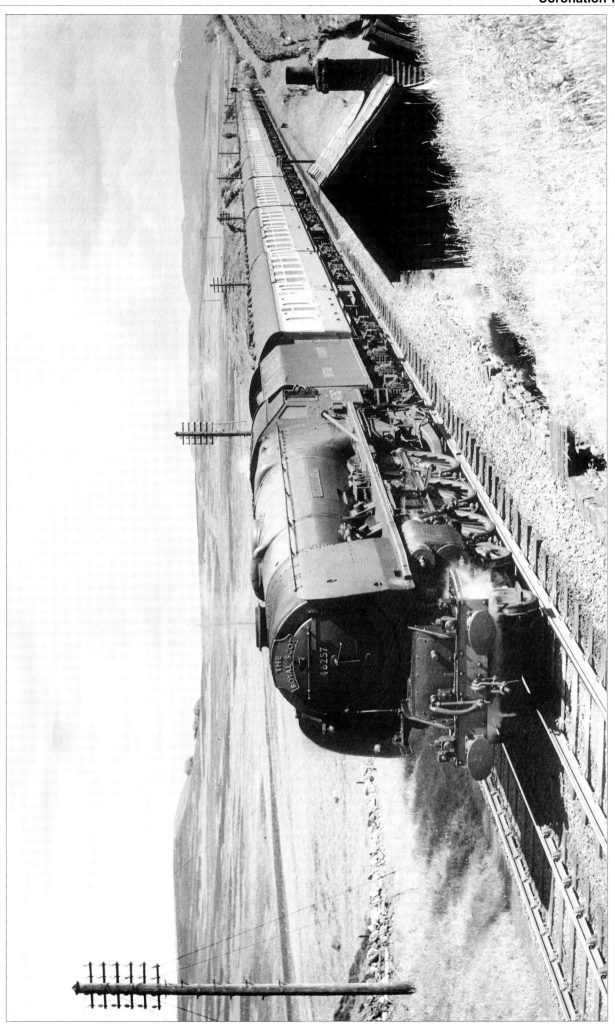

Running twelve minutes behind the Birmingham Scottish express, 46257, the last of the Coronations (though with respect to the good people of Salford it didn't carry the most stirring of names) 46257 CITY OF SALFORD nears Shap summit at about 25mph with The Royal Scot. This is 6 June 1952 and the engine still carries its electric lights, visible as a row above the buffer beam. These apparently were never satisfactory and were later removed. Photograph E.D. Bruton.

The new rear end, redesigned to accommodate the new Delta truck and the new hopper ash pan. It took something away from the 'traditional' look of the Coronations but gave them a more business-like appearance, ready for the future. Such features as these, and details such as the reverser were, in the end, not carried on in more Coronations but instead bore fruit in the BR Standards. The little mileage recorder mounted on the leading tender axlebox is clearly visible for once; both of the final pair had these. Pity about the stripe – this is Willesden near the end, in 1964. Photograph J.G. Walmsley, B.P. Hoper Collection.

46257 CITY OF SALFORD

Built Crewe 19/5/48 cost £18,248 (engine), £3,163 (tender)
Built without streamlining

Repairs BR

[Dates in first column are from out of traffic to return to traffic; the two 'mileage' figures represent, firstly the miles accumulated since the previous General or Intermediate and secondly (the generally lower figure) the miles run up from January 1st of the year of shopping. All are recorded as taking place at Crewe unless otherwise noted. StR=St Rollox]

Dates	Weekdays Waiting	Weekdays On Works	Mileage	'Jan 1' Mileage
25/5/48-26/5/48#	-	2	-	-
11/6/48-1/7/48NC	-	18	1,501	1,501
15/9/48-26/10/48NC	-	36	21,085	21,085
7/1/49-15/1/49#	-	8	-	-
15/9/49-14/10/49LC	-	26	106,546	69,811
25/2/50-3/4/50LI	-	31	138,157	12,981
24/7/50-7/11/50HC	-	91	36,776	49,757
8/11/50-11/11/50NC	-	3	36,776	49,757
12/2/51-6/3/51NC	1	18	51,722	1,751
21/5/51-2/7/51LI	9	27	76,124	26,153
1/11/51-17/1/52LC	6	58	33,929	60,082
28/1/52-30/1/52NC	-	2	35,689	1,751
6/2/52-1/3/52NC	5	16	35,680	1,751
28/3/52-8/5/52LC*	-	34	41,662	7,733
26/9/52-10/12/52HG	1	63	75,084	41,155
28/8/53-12/10/53LC	10	28	67,396	62,557
15/10/53-28/10/53NC*	-	11	67,396	62,557
8/9/54-11/10/54HI	-	28	142,486	57,589
13/10/54-26/10/54NC*	-	11	309	57,898
16/2/55-22/3/55LC*	4	25	30,258	13,148
13/10/55-26/11/55HG	-	38	79,448	62,338
5/1/57-19/2/57HI	8	22	96,641	1,263
3/12/57-24/1/58LI	8	35	66,042	67,305
1/1/59-13/3/59HG	8	43	83,621	1,155
22/3/59-25/4/59LC*	8	20	597	1,752
13/7/59-6/8/59NC*	7	14	18,975	20,130
4/9/59-24/10/59HC	12	31	27,472	28,627
7/1/60-8/2/60NC*	3	22	40,980	825
11/3/60-28/4/60LC*	22	18	49,645	9,490
27/10/60-16/12/60LI	10	33	84,179	44,024

#'no repair'
record ends
*='(EO)'- Engine Only

Sheds

Camden	22/5/48
Western Region	28/1/56
Camden	18/2/56
Carlisle Upperby	27/9/58
Stored 30/12/63-16/3/64	

Tenders

No	Fitted
10624	19/5/48

Boilers

Fitted	No.	From
19/5/48	12474	new
10/12/52	12473	-
26/11/55	13044	-
13/3/59	12474	-

Tired and travel-stained, 46257 CITY OF SALFORD, at Kingmoor in 1963. The picture, apart from being another of those striking 'side-on' images, is noteworthy for one unexpected detail difference. On the other Coronations the BR AWS Battery Box was positioned conventionally on the right-hand footplate, immediately in front of the cab. On the two last ones, with their foreshortened cab sheets, another site was found—on the left-hand side, but slung underneath the cab, as here. photograph Gavin Morrison.

LMS 'Summary' *(this became 'Annual Statistics' from 1951)*

Year	Mileage	Weekdays out of service			
		wks	shed	n/req	total
1948	36,735	-	72	1	73
1949	88,441	26	72	2	100
1950	62,952	125	24	-	149
1951	60,082	85	61	-	146
1952	45,994	115	49	-	164
1953	80,058	49	57	-	106
1954	74,699	39	59	-	98
1955	70,912	67	36	11	114
1956	86,804	-	73	-	73
1957	67,305	51	87	-	138
1958	82,466	22	66	1	89
1959	41,310			*record ends*	

wks=heavy and light repairs at main works
shed=shed repairs and examinations
n/req= not required

Total Recorded Mileage 797,758
Withdrawn week ending 12/9/64
Cut up West of Scotland
Shipbreaking Co, Troon 12/64

Saved by the holiday habit.

An Appendix
From the Horse's Mouth

A sight to make the ablest fitter groan. 6223 PRINCESS ALICE looking very down at heel, at Willesden 24 March 1945. This was the 'nuisance' value of streamlining—all that effort just to conduct a straightforward 'valve and piston' job. Photograph H.C. Casserley.

The Coronations ran great distances, given the running ground of the West Coast. With high mileage came frequent works visits and a glance at the histories will show that for any individual locomotive, it was an unusual year indeed that it did not enter Crewe Works. The high mileages (good) had the curious effect of bringing about more frequent works visits and thus lowering the availability (bad). This was only generally perceived by about Ivatt's time, hence the drive for 100,000 miles a year with roller bearings and all the labour saving devices.

Come the end of the War, in 1945, availability was 63% for English Coronations and 55% for the Scottish ones. The postponed maintenance of the War years would have contributed to this, for sure, but they were still disappointing figures. Figures under BR steadily increased but the magical 100,000 a year loco remained over the horizon, in large part, it must be said, because of the difficulties of rostering the engines to cover such distances.

The two diesels, 10000 and 10001 remained an awkward reminder of the sort of mileages that could be possible. The diesels, for

instance, would have literally eaten The Caledonian schedule with its eight coaches but the Coronations were kept on it throughout the 1950s, more or less until the end. It was even worked out that 10000 and 10001, working in tandem as they did, could manage *three* return trips to Glasgow in 24 hours, though permission to try this was never forthcoming. Ivatt ordered Polmadie to pull out the stops in an effort to get a Coronation doing two return trips in a day Euston to Glasgow but despite blokes with asbestos suits at Polmadie, trying to emulate the Americans, it did not prove feasible.

Repair categories were 'Heavy' or 'Light', according to the restorative work that would be done. Anything involving a boiler change was 'Heavy'; the category would also apply if new cylinders/tyres/tubes were fitted together with motion and brakework. Any single item undergoing repair or replacement—cylinders, tyres, tubes, motion or brakes—constituted a Light Repair, though the category usually included any number of other incidental repairs. Both these categories seemed capable of shading and grading into one another almost infinitely. The whole process, driven by costs, was

evolving right through the LMS period and into BR times, when it was to some extent standardised among the Regions. The following is a view of repairs and shopping from 1938, and fascinating for that. It was read by one H. Fowler at the Chief Mechanical Engineer's Department Annual Conference on 16 February 1938 (RAIL 418/184 at the Public Record Office). *Sir Henry* Fowler had retired five years before this and died in October 1938; the H. Fowler is presumably his son?

THE SHOPPING OF LOCOMOTIVES
PRIVATE AND NOT
FOR PUBLICATION
By H. Fowler

The Chief Mechanical Engineer being responsible for the maintenance of the Company's locomotive stock, is also responsible for deciding when an engine should receive a repair in any of the Works and also what form that repair shall take.

In order to enable him to arrive at a decision as to whether the condition of the engine is such that it should receive a repair in one of the Company's Works or whether, with or without certain routine attention at the Running Sheds, it can remain in service for a further period, he is dependent upon the information given on the Shopping proposal forms submitted by the Motive Power Section and the Boiler Inspection reports of his own Boiler Inspectors.

In considering the question of whether an engine requires a repair it is necessary to deal with it as consisting of two distinct units - the boiler and the mechanical portion - the condition of either having a direct bearing on when the whole shall be called into the Works for repairs.

As has been mentioned above, the boiler is under the direct inspection of the Chief Mechanical Engineer, through his Boiler Inspectors, and it is not proposed to deal with this unit in any detail but to consider rather the mechanical portion of the locomotive.

At the present time it is the practice for engines to be proposed for shopping after they have been in traffic for a certain period which varies for the different power classes. This method of proposing engines has many advantages from a shopping point of view for it should enable a forecast to be made of when any engine is likely to be in the Shops; in fact it should be possible to work out an annual programme for each Works. It has, however, one very great disadvantage which outweighs all the advantages in that it assumes that all engines in the same class run the same weekly mileage and that the mileage is the same summer and winter, neither of which applies in actual practice. The general result of this is that the first proposals are due before the engine has run sufficient miles to put it into such a condition that it requires workshops attention, and it has become the rule rather than the exception for the forms to be sent back for re-proposal at a later date. There are of course cases of engines running exceptional mileages which necessitate special proposal forms being submitted before the first proposal date but these are not common. It would therefore appear that some other method of arriving at the time at which the first proposal should be submitted is worth consideration, and it is suggested that the mileage run would form a more reliable basis than months in service.

Unfortunately the boiler is at work when the engine is stationary, and the hours in steam do not bear any relationship to the miles run. Any alteration to the engine proposal periods need not however affect the boiler as this is regularly reported on and special proposal forms could be called for should any defect be noted.

If the average mileage obtained between General repairs is taken out it will be found that this is approximately 120,000 miles and that engines receive a Service repair at 60,000 miles. From this is will be seen that engines which receive a valve and piston examination at 30/36,000 miles should come into the Works for every other examination, and it would appear that the same thing will apply to those engines which have an

Last touches to 46256 SIR WILLIAM A STANIER FRS, parked by the shed's 'pokers and prickers' at Camden—about 1950. Photograph Alec Swain/B.P. Hoper Collection.

extended examination period of 40/45,000 miles owing to the greater mileage being obtained between repairs. This would mean that there would be two shopping periods which would cover all classes of engine.

1. All engines receiving a valve and piston examination at 40/45,000 miles - 80,000 miles
2. All engines receiving a valve and piston examination at 30/38,000 miles - 60,000 miles

This would mean that before the second valve and piston examination was carried out proposal forms would be submitted to the Chief Mechanical Engineer, who

would decide whether this work should be done in the Sheds or the engine brought to the Works for repairs.

In cases where the condition of engines after running these mileages is such that they are still fit for service, further proposal forms would be called for after a further mileage instead of at a certain date as at present.

The actual decision as to whether an engine should be endorsed for the Shops or given a further period in traffic is based on the information given on the proposal form and the Boiler Inspector's report after the latter has been endorsed by the Chief Boiler Inspector.

The engine proposal form made out by the District Locomotive Superintendents should be an accurate report on the condition of the mechanical portion of the locomotive, if it is to be of any assistance to the person responsible for arriving at a fair decision as regards

shopping. The information entered on the form should, in reality, be a brief report of a special examination carried out by a competent person in the same way that the Boiler report is the result of a special inspection by the Boiler Inspector. Although this appears to be appreciated in many cases, quite a number of forms are received which are not satisfactory. The following cases illustrate this point:

1. A 2-6-4 Tank was proposed for Shops in the middle of November and the condition of frames was shewn as - Radial brackets and all spring hangers to renew; all brake hangers to rebush; back buffer beam bent. When the engine arrived at the Works a fortnight later it was found that the left frame was fractured right through at the driving horns.

2. Special proposal forms were called for engines of the same Class stationed at a certain Shed. When these arrived they were identical word for word although there was a large variation in the mileage.

3. An engine was proposed for Shops and mention made on the form of certain broken details. After being shopped and running its full period, it was duly proposed and the form then received was a copy of the previous one including the reporting of the broken parts.

It would appear that in the first case the examination had not been very thorough as the fracture could easily be seen when walking by the engine and in the other two cases it is doubtful if any examination had been made at all.

Another point with regard to the proposal forms is the frequent use of the

expression 'To examine', which is little if any guide to the actual condition of the part mentioned.

The accurate measurement of tyre wear, in spite of there being a standard gauge for this purpose, appears to provide a difficulty. A number of cases which have been checked have shewn a decided error, some shewing less wear than stated on the form and others more. There are a number of forms in existence which shew that the total wear has become less as more miles are run and which give the impression of insufficient care being taken in obtaining particulars.

It is felt that if it were generally appreciated that the completed form has to be used as a guide to the condition of the engine by someone possibly 400 miles away from the Shed, then greater care might be taken in seeing that the information is accurate. The bottom portion of the form is set aside for the

Coronation Pacifics

District Locomotive Superintendent to give his reasons for the recommendation he makes at the top of the form but full advantage does not seem to be taken of this. Extracts from the Boiler Inspector's report are often inserted but as both reports are examined together this is unnecessary. The sectionised part of the form covers the main portion of the engine but there are generally other items which require mention and which affect the ability of the engine to work its booked class of train. These and any other matters which are likely to be of assistance in arriving at a shopping decision should be entered in the bottom portion, which should form a summary of the engine's mechanical condition.

The question of the nature of the repair which should be given to an engine when it is in the Works is one which would appear to merit consideration. Until recently it has been the practice to deal with a Service repair as a wheel and box job, very much on the lines of the old No.4 Repair carried out at the Running Sheds. At a General Repair the engine was stripped completely to the bare frames irrespective of the condition of the details. The introduction of limits of wear saved a certain amount of unnecessary work being done after stripping but, it is suggested, overlooked one fact. If the average mileage run by engines between any two classified repairs is taken out it will be found that the distance run from a General repair to a Service is substantially the same as that between a Service repair and a General. In other words, whenever an engine is returned to traffic it will run the same mileage before being in the Shops again irrespective of the type of repair it

has received. It is therefore difficult to understand why there should be two types of limit to be worked to, one for a General Repair and the other for a Service, for if it is agreed that an engine is fit to run from a Service Repair to a General with a certain amount of wear, then, the mileage to be run being the same, it appears reasonable to suggest that the same amount of wear will carry it from a General to a Service repair without risk of failure.

It may be argued that there are certain vital parts which although they do not require actual repair have to be stripped for examination for flaws at General repairs. This cannot be avoided but the work entailed in doing this is so small that it should add very little to the cost of the repair.

If we leave the boiler out of consideration it will be found that on each occasion on which an engine comes into the Works for a repair, other than a casual, the following parts receive attention:-
Wheels and boxes
Valves and pistons
Motion
Brake gear
Frames

Apart from the boiler mountings, these parts cover almost everything on the engine which is likely to wear whilst in service. This means that apart from the periodical routine inspections in the Running sheds they are subject to Shop examination at approximately 60,000 mile periods, and it is suggested that this knowledge should be made use of in deciding what parts should be renewed at each repair rather than assume that as an engine is in for a General repair or

rather a repair to be classified as a General, everything should be brought back to standard irrespective of whether or not it would run a further 60,000 miles without replacement. The main essential in operating this scheme is that the Initial Examiners must differentiate between repairing a detail so that it will run 60,000 miles and letting it go out as it came in. There is a definite temptation to have details repaired whilst they are disconnected from an engine for inspection, which if not overcome leads to everything being repaired every time and increases the cost of repairs. An Examiner of experience, however, soon gets to know the amount of wear which may be expected to take place between shoppings and can decide quickly and surely which parts may be allowed to go.

Many moving parts of a locomotive, in common with any other machine, appear to wear fairly rapidly in the early stages of their life, after which the rate of wear slows down, there being no noticeable increase for a considerable time. Providing that the efficiency of the engine is not reduced by this wear there does not seem to be any great advantage in restoring all clearances to normal each time the engine is in the Works, as the work then done will be rapidly undone when the engine is returned to traffic, and it will probably run the majority of its working life in that condition. It is not suggested that the standard of workmanship should in any way be reduced, but rather that a number of details which at the present time are restored to normal clearances each time the engine is in the Works, might be allowed to run for a further period as any increase in wear will be so slow as to be almost negligible.

Access to the steam pipes was made by unbolting a section of the smoke deflector, moving it out of the way and, in this case at least, securing it with a single bolt at the corner. That heavy plate could easily get caught in the wind and fall off, and doubtless this practice had evolved in the light of painful experience. Photograph Alec Swain/B.P. Hoper Collection.

You'll Remember those Black and White Days...

Camden shed had 46229 DUCHESS OF HAMILTON for a long period, between June 1952 and September 1960 when it moved to Crewe North. Here it is at Polmadie shed on 27 June 1953, turned with its tender topped up ready for the journey south. The valve gear is set in forward, so unless it is about to move off somebody should be due for a dressing down! It was always drilled into enginemen; *regulator closed, engine in middle gear, handbrake on, boiler full, taps open, dampers shut* when leaving engines. The Royal Scot behind, 46154 THE HUSSAR, was also Camden based at the time and while the Pacific might have come north on a through working from London, it is doubtful if the Scot would have done, so this engine could well have been on a cyclic diagram. One of the sheds grimy Austerity 2-8-0s is visible to the right. Photograph W. Hermiston, www.transporttreasury.co.uk

CITY OF HEREFORD standing in Carlisle station on 6 October 1962. With class one headlamps it is doubtless waiting for an up train to arrive from Glasgow which it will take forward. Allocated to the Border City it will in all probability take the train through to Euston. Photograph Paul Chancellor Collection.